Edward de Bono has had faculty appointments at the universities of Oxford, London, Cambridge and Harvard. He is widely regarded as the leading authority in the direct teaching of thinking as a skill. He originated the concept of lateral thinking and developed formal techniques for deliberate creative thinking. He has written fifty-seven books, which have been translated into thirty-four languages, has made two television series and there are over 4,000,000 references to his work on the Internet.

Dr de Bono has been invited to lecture in fifty-two countries and to address major international conferences. In 1989 he was asked to chair a special meeting of Nobel Prize laureates. His instruction in thinking has been sought by some of the leading business corporations in the world such as IBM, Du Pont, Shell, Eriksson, McKinseys, Ciba-Geigy, Ford and many others. He has had a planet named after him by the International Astronomic Union and was named by a group of university professors in South Africa as one of the 250 people in all of history who have contributed most to humanity.

Dr de Bono runs the most widely used programme for the direct teaching of thinking in schools. This is now in use in many countries around the world.

Dr de Bono's key contribution has been his understanding of the brain as a self-organizing system. From this solid base he set out to design practical tools for thinking. His work is in use equally in the boardrooms of some of the world's largest corporations and with four-year-olds in school. His design of the Six Hats method provides, for the first time, Western thinking with a constructive idiom instead of adversarial argument. His work is in use in élite gifted schools, rural schools in South Africa and Khmer villages in Cambodia. The appeal of Dr de Bono's work is its simplicity and practicality.

For more information about Dr de Bono's public seminars, private seminars, certified training programmes, thinking programmes for schools, CD Rom, books and tapes, please contact: Diane McQuaig, The McQuaig Group, 132 Rochester Avenue, Toronto M4N 1P1, Ontario, Canada. Tel: (416) 488 0008. Fax: (416) 488 4544. Internet: http://www.edwdebono.com/

TITLES PUBLISHED IN PENGUIN

Atlas of Management Thinking
Conflicts: A Better Way to Resolve Them
Edward de Bono's Masterthinker's Handbook
Edward de Bono's Textbook of Wisdom
The 5-Day Course in Thinking
Handbook for the Positive Revolution
The Happiness Purpose
How to be More Interesting
I Am Right You Are Wrong
Lateral Thinking
Lateral Thinking for Management
Opportunities
Parallel Thinking
Po: Beyond Yes and No
Practical Thinking
Simplicity
Six Thinking Hats
Teach Your Child How to Think
Teach Yourself to Think
Teaching Thinking
The Use of Lateral Thinking
Water Logic
Wordpower

New Thinking for the New Millennium

Edward de Bono

PENGUIN BOOKS

PENGUIN BOOKS

Published by the Penguin Group
Penguin Books Ltd, 27 Wrights Lane, London W8 5TZ, England
Penguin Putnam Inc., 375 Hudson Street, New York, New York 10014, USA
Penguin Books Australia Ltd, Ringwood, Victoria, Australia
Penguin Books Canada Ltd, 10 Alcorn Avenue, Toronto, Ontario, Canada M4V 3B2
Penguin Books (NZ) Ltd, Private Bag 102902, NSMC, Auckland, New Zealand

Penguin Books Ltd, Registered Offices: Harmondsworth, Middlesex, England

First published by Viking 1999
Published in Penguin Books 2000
1 3 5 7 9 10 8 6 4 2

Copyright © The McQuaig Group Inc., 1999
All rights reserved

The moral right of the author has been asserted

Set in Monotype Baskerville
Typeset by Rowland Phototypesetting Ltd, Bury St Edmunds, Suffolk
Printed in England by Clays Ltd, St Ives plc

Everything has changed except our way of thinking.
Albert Einstein

Is it too late to change our way of thinking?
Edward de Bono

This book is written according to the mathematical theory of dispersed cross-sensitivity (in a self-organizing system). Roughly speaking this means that water flowing down a river does less for the land than rain falling widely over the area. That is why the Grand Canyon cuts through a desert. For that reason the paragraphs in the first part of this book have been randomized. As you proceed through the paragraphs it is more like proceeding through the experiences of life than walking down a pathway set for you.

People who are constipated become irritable, grumpy and bad-tempered. It is time we moved on from the constipated judgemental thinking of the last millennium and all the strife it caused, to thinking which is more concerned with design and value creation.

You can analyse the past but you need to design the future.

That is the difference between suffering the future and enjoying it.

The Diagrams

Just as the paragraphs in the first part of the text are deliberately random so also are the diagrams. The diagrams do not reflect the adjacent text – each diagram exists in its own right. Experience has shown that while some readers appreciate the visual message of a diagram, other readers tend to get irritated by diagrams. The important point is not to seek to work out a diagram in great detail but to use the diagram as an overall reinforcement of points made somewhere in the text. This visual illustration parallels the written one.

The figures in the diagrams are stylized tadpoles – even if some readers choose to see them as spermatozoa. Because these tadpoles are hardly lifelike they will be called 'toles'.

A tole has a direction of movement which is opposite to the propelling tail. The toles are usually shown in a two-dimensional world. It is a paradox that two-dimensional worlds are more realistic than three-dimensional worlds because the two-dimensional world can more easily show relationships, movement, progress, etc. The third dimension only adds confusion.

The toles are simple to draw and obvious to view – which is why this particular shape was chosen.

If you have to struggle to understand a particular diagram – then don't! The diagrams are intended to make things clearer, not to make the reader work harder.

If there is a known and successful cure for an illness, the patient would much prefer the doctor to use this cure rather than seek to design a better one. Yet there may be much better cures. How are they ever to be developed if at each moment the traditional treatment must be preferred? It is little wonder that the judgement mode of the last millennium restricts us to past successes if the matter is important. Design is at best a risky process but without design there is no progress.

1

'Everything is fine. But the ship is still heading in the wrong direction.'

There are hundreds of companies and thousands of people writing software for computers. What about the human computer? What about the human brain? How many people are writing software for the human brain? Not many at all. Why is that? Is it that we know that our existing thinking habits are so perfect that they are beyond improvement? Is it that we cannot imagine any different or better thinking habits? Is it that we are so very complacent? Is it that it would be so immensely difficult to introduce any new thinking? If you lived in a remote part of France without radio, television, pop music or tourists, would it occur to you that there might be languages other than French? Even if it did occur to you, would you believe that another language might be 'better' in some way: more precise, more expressive, more economical, etc.? The answer must surely be no. When you are within a system, when that system serves you very well, when everyone around you is in the same system, then it is very hard to imagine any alternatives. We have got so used to our existing mental software that we see no fault or limitation in it. We cannot see why it should ever need changing. And yet, in the last few decades, it has been shown that different thinking habits can be very much more powerful. For example the 'parallel thinking' of the Six Hats system is very much faster and more effective than our traditional argument system. Meeting times can be reduced to one quarter or even one tenth. That is why this new software is being used both by major corporations around the world and also by four-year-olds in schools.

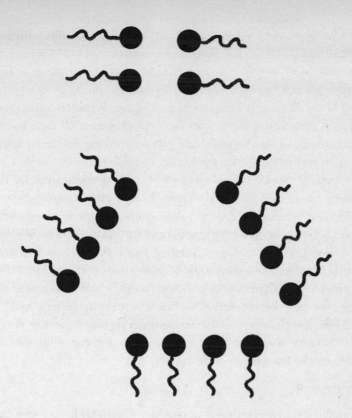

Parallel Thinking

The top part of the drawing shows the usual 'argument' or adversarial thinking, in which each side seeks to attack the other side. The bottom part shows parallel thinking, in which at every moment all thinkers are looking in the same direction. These directions will then change – as with the Six Hats framework.

It is possible for a system to evolve to the point where further evolution is no longer possible. The system comes to fit the existing circumstances so well that any change would be negative at first – even if it was beneficial in the long run. Evolution gives a better and better fit to existing circumstances, but if the circumstances change then that good fit can be a disadvantage. If the climate warmed up, those animals that had evolved long fur might suffer from hyperthermia. With evolution, changes in circumstances are not usually met by the adaptation of existing species but by the emergence of new species which fit the new circumstances better. Education is a prime example of a system that has evolved to the point where it is no longer capable of further evolution. What is provided by education gets further and further away from the needs of society and the needs of individuals within society. For example, education is obsessed with literacy and numeracy. Yet 'operacy' (the skills of doing) is almost entirely neglected. As soon as a youngster leaves school that youngster is going to need operacy. The Socratic idea 'that knowledge is all' is nonsense unless it also includes the knowledge of doing.

●━━━━━━━●

Imagine a ship at sea that is in trouble. The lights keep going out. The engine is faltering. The rudder is unreliable. The first mate is drunk. The crew is very demoralized. The service is appalling. The passengers on the ship are very dissatisfied. Then a new captain and first mate are brought in by helicopter. Very quickly everything changes. The morale of the crew is lifted. Service improves. The engine is fixed. The rudder is fixed. The lights stay on. Everything is fine. But the ship is still heading in the wrong direction. That is usually the case when we set out to fix things. We might be very successful in fixing things within the existing context (or direction) but it does not occur to us that the basic context may need fixing. You can have a street that is muddy and full of puddles. You put a lot of people to work keeping that street clean. But it might have made more sense to fix the drainage

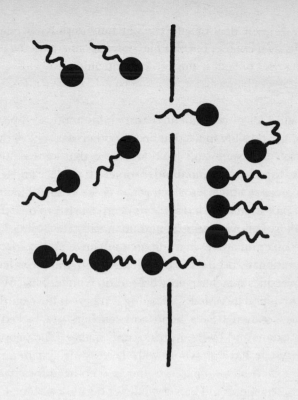

The Academic Game

Take in the information. Store the information in a neat and organized way. When asked, give back the information in an ordered and structured manner. Some people are not good at this particular game – but are far from stupid.

instead. A great deal of effort is put into improving education within its own context but this may have no effect whatsoever on changing the context or direction of education.

●━━━━━●

There are a lot of very talented and highly motivated people in education – possibly more than in any other sector. Yet they are locked into a system and have to follow that system. In most countries there are examinations of some sort in place and teachers have to prepare students to get through those exams. That is what parents expect; that is what students need in order to pass through the gateways into a successful and financially rewarding life. Yet the examinations are set in traditional subjects. The examinations have traditionally been set by universities. Both traditional subjects and universities may have very little to do with real life. Where is the examination in 'practical thinking'? Where is the examination in 'value creation'? So schools and teachers are locked in by existing exams and by the needs of universities. The people who run the system have grown up with the existing system and have become experts at running it, so they see no need for change. In any case, change would be very difficult because a change in any one part would put that part out of synchrony with all other parts. So goodwill and a sense of the need for change come to nothing.

●━━━━━●

Education is like a pyramid. Everyone at the bottom of the pyramid is taught so that the top 20 per cent (or more) go on to university. The 80 per cent that do not make it to university are 'rejects'. What they have been taught has been to get them into a fit shape to pass the exams and get into university. Much of this has very little value in the world outside. So they have been trained to run a race but if they do not qualify for that particular race then their training is not of much use to them elsewhere.

●━━━━━●

Education is a sort of pyramid. The purpose is to bring out the more able youngsters, who will then go on to university and provide the skills and leadership which society needs. Perhaps we could turn the system around. Perhaps all students should primarily be taught 'life skills', such as operacy, basic thinking, value creation, etc. The more able and more academically inclined would then be able to take a special stream that would flow on to university. This is equivalent to teaching everyone to walk and then giving special coaching to those who showed an ability to run. This is different from the present system of coaching everyone to run and then neglecting those who are not good at running.

The 'academic game' is a very special game. You are required to take in and to remember quite a lot of information. You have to store this. Then, on demand, as in examinations, you are required to sort through the stored information and to give it back. Youngsters who are poor on the input or storage side have no chance at all in the academic game. In my experience, however, these youngsters may be very good thinkers. If they are asked to think about something which does not depend on stored knowledge, they perform very well. Indeed, in the 'thinking lessons', such youngsters surprise their teachers and their classmates. A boy who was regarded as 'dumb' is suddenly seen to be a very good thinker.

You have an excellent road map. Once you know the road map you can figure out how to get to most places using the existing roads. Knowledge of the existing world, and judgement to check that knowledge, allows us to use existing methods. But knowing a road map does not construct new roads. The past millennium of recognition, judgement, discrimination allows us to use our knowledge but does not help to design new possibilities.

2

Is it possible that one day dominance by aggression will be replaced by 'dominance by wisdom'?

(Dulini Game Reserve in South Africa; having got up at six in the morning to go out to see two dominant male lions and, later, two lionesses feeding five cubs)

With baboons there is a 'general' who dominates a troop of thirty baboons. Below the general are four or five enforcers who see that the will of the general gets carried out. Mothers scold and cuff their children if they do not behave. Senior females who do not have babies steal a baby from another female. The baby dies because there is no milk.

●————————●

Lions are very social animals. Two male lions will bond to dominate a territory. Sometimes as many as five lions form a consortium. Females will happily suckle the cubs of a friend. So there is a strong sense of territory and dominance, but also of cooperation.

●————————●

The animal kingdom is full of 'dominance'. Usually it is a male that is dominant, occasionally a female. This dominance is achieved by force and reinforced later by the threat of force. Such dominance obviously has an organizing value in animals that live in social groups. It also has a species-survival value. The toughest and most aggressive animals get to be dominant and then do most of the mating. So the genes for toughness and aggression get widely spread. In the bird world, where aggression is not so important, mating is on the basis of 'vanity'. The good-looking male gets the attention of the ladies. So the genes for good looks get spread around. It is also possible that these are really the genes for good health, as an unhealthy bird does not look very handsome. Dominance in human society is also achieved by force and

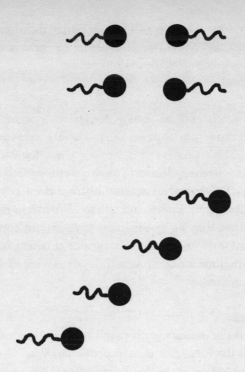

Constructive Thinking

Instead of confrontational thinking (top part), there is an attempt to build on everyone's contribution and so to progress forward.

aggression, or by the rule of law operating through a political system. Democracy tries to suggest that in the end it is 'the people's choice' that is going to achieve dominance.

●━━━━━━●

Democracy often evolves into a two-party system: those that propose and those that oppose. Why not have everyone involved in the constructive process of designing a way forward? Because it would be far too complicated to have a way forward that satisfied most people. This may be because we have been cultured in the either/or habit of argument and debate. We are so used to win/lose as an idiom that we assume that if we do not completely get our own way then we have 'lost'. So our thinking habits create the system and then we claim that the system is inevitable because of our thinking habits.

●━━━━━━●

The basic idea of democracy is that one party wins and the other loses. This is the most practical approximation to 'the will of the people'. Where there is the possibility of a change in government, some people are satisfied some of the time and the others at another time. Where there is a permanent minority, as in Northern Ireland, then some people are never going to be in power.

●━━━━━━●

Democracy can certainly be redesigned and improved in many ways. One possibility is to compensate the losers. If your party loses in an election, then you are compensated by paying 10 per cent less tax than someone who voted for the winning party. Some system of party or vote registration would be needed. Whenever I have suggested this idea, those people belonging to a likely winning party have hated the idea. Any change that is not going to benefit the likely ruling party is not very likely to happen.

●━━━━━━●

Could the adversarial nature of traditional democracy ever be replaced by joint constructive thinking, just as argument is being replaced by the parallel thinking of the Six Hats method? I do think it is possible, on the basis of the 'best design of the way forward'. But who is to choose the best design? With today's interactive technology (possibly through the TV set) it is easier than ever before to have the best design chosen either by popular choice or by a 'jury'.

●——————●

Is it possible that one day dominance by aggression will be replaced by 'dominance by wisdom'? Is it possible in any system that ultimately depends on popular choice, that this popular choice would be sufficiently wise to make the right choice (for all parties, and long-term as well as short-term)? I believe it is possible, but only if we teach thinking in all schools and from an early age. There is no existing school subject that is more important. There is no subject that is more neglected.

●——————●

Suppose that in a parliament of two hundred and ten seats, one party has one hundred seats and the other party has eighty. There would be a 'virtual party' of thirty seats (the formula for the number can be varied but could be about one seventh of the total number of seats). This virtual party would have no sitting members. These virtual seats would be voted by opinion polls. If the government proposed something and the opposition disagreed, than an opinion poll would be held on the issue. If 70 per cent of those polled were against the suggestion then twenty-one seats would vote with the opposition and the proposal would fail. Conversely, if the opposition suggested something and the opinion polls showed that 70 per cent of those polled supported this opposition suggestion, then this would become law. So the opposition could also introduce legislation at any point and not only when in government. In technical matters, such as economics, these seats might be voted by a technical panel. Anyone could apply to join this technical panel but would have to pass some sort of test in economics.

———•———

The brain is specifically designed to be non-creative. The brain is designed to adjust to a stable world. The brain is a self-organizing environment in which incoming information organizes itself into patterns. Once those patterns are formed then all the brain needs to do is to recognize the pattern and then follow along the track. It is through the use of these established routine patterns that we cope so well with the complex world.

———•———

Once upon a time someone set up his computer to calculate how long it would take to get dressed if there were eleven items of clothing to be put on. The computer was probably working at 80 megahertz at the time. The computer took forty hours of non-stop working. This is not surprising. With eleven items of clothing there are 39,916,800 way of getting dressed. If you spent one minute on each way, you would need to live to be seventy-six years old to go through each way. The mathematics are simple: there are eleven choices for the first item, ten for the next, nine for the next ($11 \times 10 \times 9 \times 8 \times 7$, etc. or factorial 11). Since there are other things to do with our lives apart from just getting dressed, we should be immensely grateful that the brain sets up routine patterns and then uses them.

———•———

A pattern is like a path. When you are on a path, the next stop is more likely to be along that path than in any other direction. You are less likely to step off the path or go back along the path. In the same way, a particular state of the neurones in the brain is more likely to be followed by another specific state than by a random state. So the brain moves smoothly from one state to the next state – that is what following a pattern is all about.

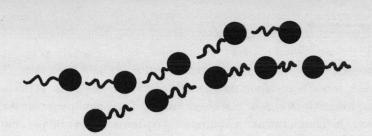

Win/Lose

The two streams meet. One stream dominates and suppresses the other. There are winners and losers. This is our more usual way of settling differences.

The downside of patterns is that once we have set them up we are trapped by them. Once streams and rivers have been formed, then water flows along those established channels – the water is no longer free to flow elsewhere and to form new patterns. We have no choice but to use established patterns for over 90 per cent of our thinking and our behaviour. But we also need the ability to challenge these patterns from time to time in order to set up better patterns.

'What is this?' It is obvious that judgement has to be the core activity of the brain. An animal needs to recognize which berries are good to eat and which are poisonous. An animal needs to recognize predators and their shapes, sounds and smells. A baboon needs to recognize the dominant male 'general' in the troop otherwise he or she would be in trouble. As soon as the brain can recognize something then the appropriate routine patterns or response can be set off. The system is very effective and very powerful. It is also immensely practical. Quick recognition is followed by quick response. Once we recognize 'what something is' then we know about it and what it is going to do.

Judgement, recognition and identification are the basis of all biological survival behaviour. Once the organism recognizes or identifies the situation then the appropriate response can be used. There does not have to be a human-type conscious recognition with a language and naming element. The recognition can be 'hard-wired' into the organism as instinct. With instinct the response is automatic and instant.

If you hold a lighted match to a piece of newspaper, the newspaper is likely to catch fire. (I say 'likely' because the paper may be wet.) This is simply cause and effect. There is a flow through from flame on the match to burning newspaper. The newspaper does not have to 'recognize' the flame and then burst into flame. The heat is the 'flow-through' link. With people and other organisms the link might be perception in its broadest sense. The action has to fit the situation and is not random. This is where 'recognition' comes in. When someone sticks a pin into you, you say something like 'ouch' and jump away. The flow-through is as simple as cause and effect.

A skilled carpenter can turn out faithful reproductions of Sheraton and Hepplewhite furniture. This may indeed be more attractive than what is being done by contemporary designers. So how are new designs to emerge, if no one attempts them and no one buys them? The repetition habits of the last millennium are risk averse but also progress averse. The design habits of the new millennium might cause some initial problems but these would soon disappear.

3

The weakness of the judgement system is that it was never designed for change.

A doctor is in her surgery and a child is brought in with a rash. The doctor has to identify the condition in order to provide treatment and in order to predict what might happen next – and to reassure the worried mother. So the doctor looks through, in her mind, the possible patterns triggered by the visible rash. It might be sunburn. It might be allergy to food or other chemicals. It might be measles, etc. The doctor then carefully examines the signs and symptoms. The doctor takes a history as to how and when the condition occurred. All this goes into the 'recognition' or diagnostic process of the doctor. Once the doctor has made up her mind then the recognized treatment is applied and the doctor also keeps in mind possible future complications. This is the judgement system at its best. Carefully judge and recognize standard situations and then apply standard remedies (and expectations).

From our own experience and, more importantly, from the experiences of others (via books, courses, etc.) we learn about standard situations and standard ways of dealing with them. This is what education is all about.

Putting together and 'naming' standard situations is extremely important because a 'standard situation' links accumulated past experience with present action and future prediction. The establishment of an illness called 'measles' means that the doctor

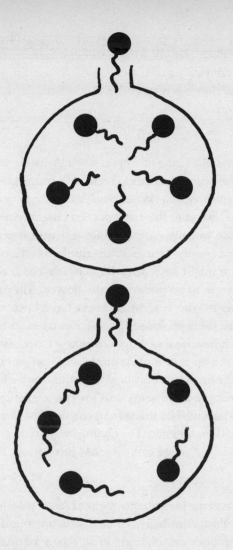

Chance or Design

In the top part the toles are all swimming in different directions. One of them finds the way out of the bottle by 'chance'. Many discoveries are indeed made by chance. In the bottom part there is an organized search procedure and this is sure to find the opening.

knows what is happening; what is likely to happen (the usual course of the illness); likely complications (like ear infection); the treatment; and the likely duration and infectivity of the condition. The system is so powerful that it is no wonder that it became the basis of our thinking habits.

As a member of the Gang of Three, it was Aristotle who laid down the basis for 'inclusion/exclusion logic'. He set up categories which were standard situations. When you came across something you had to 'judge' was it in this category, or box, or was it not in this category? Two botanists are looking at a wild flower. Each one identifies it differently. One botanist thinks it is 'flower A' but the other thinks it might be 'flower B'. Each gives his reasons based on what they see to be present in the flower. They may have an 'argument' as to who is right. Flowers have been very carefully classified over the ages (starting with Linnaeus in Sweden). It is just possible it may be a new species not yet identified. The main point about the approach of Aristotle was that something had to be in that box or not in that box. It could not be half in or half out. Nor could it be anywhere else. One can see how very powerful the certainty provided by this system can be. The doctor can make a diagnosis with confidence. The chemist can predict the behaviour of a chemical. The judge can dispense justice.

The weakness of the judgement system is that it was never designed for change. You identified standard situations and you applied standard responses or solutions (if it was a standard problem). Stable civilizations, like those in ancient Greece and Africa, saw no need for change because they had evolved to a stable state. If change happens – through science, technology, climatic conditions or value shifts – then the judgement system cannot cope. If the 'standard' situations were no longer standard, then what should the response be? Analysis seeks to come to the rescue by suggesting that the new situations can really be broken down into standard elements. Sometimes this is true, but more often the result is disastrous. Judgement is essentially a 'backward-looking' system. This is enough for most of our thinking and behaviour but we also need 'forward-looking' design and innovation.

The judgement system has its own in-built faults. We get better and quicker at judging. The doctor no longer makes a thorough examination to see if the child has measles. Instead she just looks for the characteristic 'Koplik spots'. Experts always take short cuts because they have found out what is essential and what is unnecessary. So judgements are based on single features. The result of this is stereotypes and prejudices. Whole groups are lumped together on some simple basis, enough to judge that someone belongs to that group: Jews, Catholics, Protestants, blacks, etc. The system which provides a useful basis for expertise in some areas also provides for discrimination, persecutions, injustice and pogroms.

The emotional part of 'feeling right' is very important and insufficiently explored. An Irishman once said to me: 'When I am wrong I am the first to apologize – but when I am right I will fight to the death.' That about sums up the problem in Northern Ireland. The feeling of being right has a perceptual or logical basis, but the feeling is a strong emotion. What goes on in the mind and the practical utility of 'feeling right' are not really known. It could be that this 'feeling' is necessary to stop us searching for further answers and so to help with decisions and choices. Unfortunately, others may have a different perspective and also 'feel right' very strongly.

The brain has a powerful 'mismatch' system. This means that a new perception is matched with an existing appropriate pattern. If they do not fit, there is an upset feeling. When Professor Bruner at Harvard asked people to look through a 'normal' pack of cards they were very upset to find that one of the cards was not what was expected. You would expect a three of hearts to be red and would get upset, and even nauseous, if you came across a black three of hearts in a pack which was otherwise totally normal.

●━━━━●

If we have experience, then we have expectations, because we believe we know what to expect. Judgement tells us whether what we find fits our experience. Sometimes, something does not fit our expectation but then, suddenly, we realize that it does fit another experience. Humour is like that. We are led along one path of expectation – and then suddenly switched to another which is quite logical. 'Golf clubs are not much use – unless they have swimming-pools'. The pun switches the two meanings of 'golf club'.

●━━━━●

Is there any value to speed in judgement? Obviously there are times when speed is very important. You are driving along a misty road and see a vague shape in front of you. It is important that you identify the shape as quickly as you can: is it a stationary truck; is it a trailer piled high with straw; is it a tree blown across the road, etc. You may also have to judge quickly what another motorist is up to ahead of you on any road. So there are times when speed of judgement is important. At other times we do go for speed of judgement because we do not like the uncertainty of making judgements. The quicker it is done with the better. So we seek 'completeness' by making snap judgements. We do this by focusing on a few features which we consider key (as an expert might) or by using broad pre-set stereotypes: 'All people with eyes set close together are not to be trusted.' Stereotypes give easy

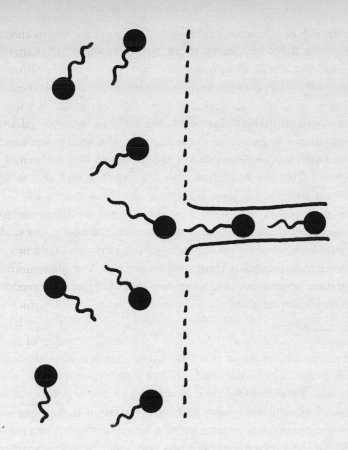

Routine

The toles are messing around wondering what to do. The 'routine'
channel provides a known, tried and tested way of moving forward.
Routines are excellent and practical – but not enough.

judgements. In all cases where speed of judgement is not essential, judgements should probably be as slow as possible. That allows full consideration of all factors.

●————————●

We do need to make judgements. We need to see what part of our experience is applicable at the moment. We need to see which stored patterns can be used. We do not want to have to work things out from the beginning. So if we cannot find an exactly matching pattern, we look for similarity: 'This is very like . . .' That allows us to deal with new things until we have enough experience of them to set up a new pattern. 'Similarity' extends the usefulness of our existing stock of patterns. The difficulty is when we treat as similar things which are not. The phrase 'That is the same as what we are doing now' has killed more new ideas than any other comment.

●————————●

The major advantage of the judgement system is also its major disadvantage. The boxes, categories or stereotypes are very pure. They are 'fixed models' or examples. The doctor's concept of measles has to be the classic concept. Variation is not possible. Your imagining of the capital letter A is very definite. The system could not work otherwise. So when you 'judge' something into a box that something is completely in the box. You no longer respond to what is before you but to the classic, fixed model. At its extreme, this is the basis of stereotypes, prejudices, etc. Even if we consciously avoid such extremes, we may still miss the particular variations of what is in front of us.

●————————●

'Fuzzy logic' was developed in the USA by a Russian immigrant called Lotfi Zadeh. As fuzzy logic was taken up, many scientific journals refused to publish anything on fuzzy logic. If fuzzy logic was included in a paper the author was asked to cut it out. This

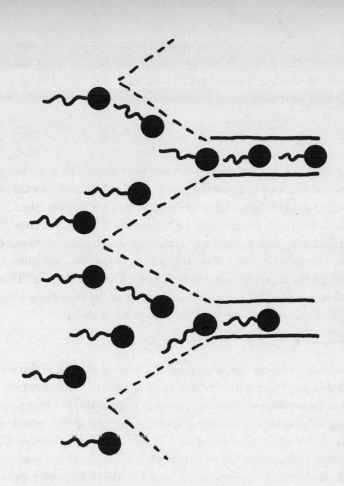

Established Patterns

The brain can only see what it is prepared to see. What is before us is
seen in terms of established patterns. This also goes for behaviour
where we respond with established patterns. We react to the new in
terms of the old.

was because fuzzy logic contradicted one of the principles of Aristotle. This principle insisted that something was either completely in the box or completely outside the box. Fuzzy logic suggested that something could be partly in the box and partly outside the box.

●━━━━━●

In the days of 'magic medicine' it was very important to recognize standard diseases because for each standard disease there was a complex composition of special herbs and even incantations. 'This is the falling sickness, so this is what we do.' This was a practical and usable system. As medicine developed and treatment became more scientific, it was still useful to keep these disease names just as botanists kept the multiple names of plants. In the future, however, it may be more useful to think of 'system faults' as we begin to understand the pathological basis of disease.

●━━━━━●

In science progress has been made by a combination of 'lumping and splitting'. Lumping means putting together things which at first appear different. So flowers which appear different are recognized as belonging to the same species. For a long time ornithologists in Australia thought that a bright red parrot was quite a different species to a bright green parrot. Finally they recognized that they were simply the male and female of the same species. 'Splitting' is the opposite process. Things which seem the same or have always been treated as being the same are now seen to be quite different. A sore throat always feels much the same to the person with a sore throat. But a good doctor will distinguish between a streptococcal sore throat, which needs treating with antibiotics, and a viral sore throat, which does not respond to antibiotics.

●━━━━━●

Judgement works on a crystallization of the past. Experiences are crystallized into words in language and standard situations. In a stable world the system gets richer and more competent all the time. We learn to discriminate more finely between situations. We improve our standard responses to identified situations. We should get progressively wiser and more clever. To a large extent we have done just this. But if the world is not stable, then these standard situations from the past may no longer describe the world around us. Is education really the same in the days of the Internet as it was before? Is industrial development the same in times of ecological sensitivity as it was before? Is democracy the same in times of mass media communication as it was before?

●———————●

We cannot judge something we do not know. The best we can do is to try to break it down into parts we do know. This is the powerful process of analysis, which so dominates education. The difficulty is that the nature of the parts may not indicate the function of the whole. A pile of small cogwheels and a spring does not tell much about the function of a clock. The individual members of a family may not indicate much about the dynamics of that family. The second way of understanding something we do not know is to compare it to something we do know. New situations are always being compared to historical precedents. Usually the comparison may seem to be plausible but often this is a superficial and misleading resemblance.

Some people, including children, are extremely good at recognizing a piece of music from the first few notes. But recognizing music does not make you a composer. Recognition is powerful and useful but it is not design. In the past millennium the domination of our thinking habits by the recognition and judgement mode was possibly justified. That dominance is no longer justified. In the next millennium we may want to be able to use our knowledge and our technology to design better ways forward.

4

Logic is not so much a
thinking mechanism as a
'communication
mechanism'.

Shiny white tiles on the bathroom wall: a kid puts a muddy handprint on the tiles. All you have to do is clean off the muddy print and everything is back to perfect. Someone has left the light on in the corridor and you cannot sleep. You get up and switch off the light: the problem has been solved and you sleep. A dishonest person is stealing money from the till: you sack that person and all is well. You have a sore throat and a high fever: your doctor prescribes penicillin and the sore throat is cured. If you can make bad things go away, then you will be left with good things. This is an obvious strategy. So we concentrate on identifying and then seeking to remove the bad things. The capitalist world thought that the Marxist system in the USSR was a bad thing. It would be enough to remove this and then Jeffersonian democracy would be restored. It did not quite work out that way. At a UN meeting in Washington two people from a developing country got up to blame everything on the multinationals. The difficulty is that sometimes it is indeed enough to remove a 'bad thing' but at other times you are left with something even worse.

●————●

Being against something is very satisfactory. There is a direction for thinking, acting and feeling. There is a defined mission. There may be companions to share your feelings. There may even be the achievement satisfaction of planting terrorist bombs. The simplicity of this thinking/behaviour is very attractive. Failure to teach constructive thinking to youngsters means that the only activity open to mentally energetic youngsters is to be against

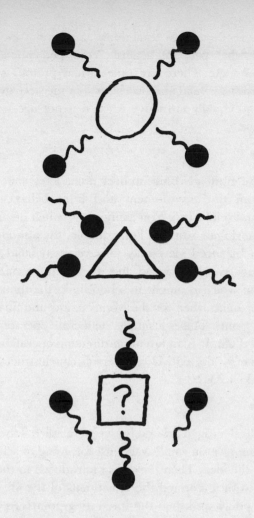

New Situations

The toles do not like the circle and move away from it. The toles are
attracted to the triangle. These are traditional and known situations.
The square is a 'new situation'. So no one knows how to respond.

everything. To be against something, you do not even need to understand what you are against. Your perception, however wrong, is enough. There are times when protest groups and revolutionaries are valid and necessary, but the strategy is equally powerful and equally attractive when it is not necessary and is unproductive.

———•————•———

Attitudes are gradually built up over time. They arise from role models, from the environment and from behaviour that is rewarded and reinforced. You cannot just switch on an attitude. You cannot 'do' an attitude. For example, the attitude involved in taking a balanced view may take years to build up. But a thinking 'tool' can be learned and used in three minutes. The PMI system which is taught in schools asks the thinker to scan for the Plus points, then for the Minus points and finally for the Interesting points. This is a simple, deliberate operation which is easily carried out. It is an attention-directing operation. You can ask someone to 'do a PMI'. A person can instruct himself or herself to 'do a PMI'.

———•————•———

Thirty youngsters aged around twelve were asked if they liked the idea of being given a small wage just for going to school. All of them liked the idea. Then they were introduced to the PMI. In small groups they scanned the Plus points of the idea and then the Minus points and then the Interesting points. At the end of this exercise twenty-nine out of thirty had changed their minds and decided it was a bad idea.

———•————•———

Our brains are full of 'description concepts' of what we see around us: car, table, house, etc. There are very few 'operational concepts' which tell us what to do at any moment. We feel it is enough just to react to what is in front of us. We react to our perception. But we have no way of ensuring that the perception is useful or real. The PMI becomes an operational concept in the mind. It has its own identity and existence. Teaching the PMI with its acronym is very much more powerful and quicker than trying to teach the attitude of a balanced view. Design the game, ask people to play the game and they will – with ease. As a result of playing the game their perceptions are much improved. As a result of better perceptions their actions and feelings are more appropriate. There is a huge difference between seeking to teach attitudes and teaching a 'thinking tool'.

In one of my books I suggest that there is a difference between 'rock logic' and 'water logic'. The logic of identity is rock logic, since this identity does not change. It is because of this unchanging base that we can move forward to conclusions. 'Water logic' is the logic of flow. Water flows forward. Flow logic is more concerned with what happens next: where does our mind flow to. Flow logic opens up possibilities but does not deliver certainties.

(HM 061 Air Seychelles flight from Johannesburg to Mahe in the Seychelles)

There is a huge difference between positive thinking and constructive thinking. You are standing in a market-place and a car parks on your foot. Positive thinking suggests that you make the best of your enforced immobility. You look around and appreciate the architecture. You watch the stallholders and human nature. You inhale and appreciate the smells. You chat to children who gather around. Constructive thinking suggests you make an effort to get the car shifted.

Positive thinking suggests adjusting to the situation and making the best of it by looking on the positive side. Constructive thinking suggests you seek to improve the situation. If there is absolutely nothing you can do then positive thinking is better than negative thinking. In general, however, the attitude of constructive thinking should prevail.

All action is either routine or based on possibilities. If you use a tried routine you have a right to expect that the routine will work this time as it has in the past. If there is no applicable routine, then you have to think up a 'possible course of action'. There is no guarantee that it will work. The 'possibility' may range from something that is very likely to work to something that is only remotely likely. When you set out to invite people to a party you are dealing with possibilities: the person invited may come or may not come. You may be fairly sure that some of the guests are going to come. With others, however, the probability is much less. In some cases there may be only a slight chance that the invited person will come.

Men are said to use logic more than women do. There may be a reason for this perception. Men have traditionally worked in groups. They went mastodon hunting in groups. They set out to fight wars in groups. They set up businesses in groups. Logic is not so much a thinking mechanism as a 'communication mechanism'. You had to convince others to go along with you. You had to think together to get an agreed outcome. Logic was essential. Women tended to work alone. So the communication function of logic was not so important. Women could rely on intuition. Logic is step-by-step processing so that everyone can follow the steps to the conclusion. Intuition is more 'field-effect' processing. Many factors are fed into the field and gradually the outcome forms itself. To carry people with you into action you have to suggest certainty. To work on your own you need only possibility.

━━━━━●━━━━━━●━━━━━

Money is a token of exchange. In the past a fisherman might exchange fish for grain from a farmer. A brothel lady in Nevada could be paid with a chicken. Money was more convenient. You were paid in money and you could then buy something with the money. In the same way there are certain 'value words', which act as tokens of value. Instead of having to explain why something will not work or having to show that something might indeed work, you use simple words like 'good' and 'bad': 'That is a bad idea'; 'That is a good idea.' 'Good' and 'bad' are token words which are accepted as indicating value. Just as a person with too much money can become a spendthrift, so the very existence of these value words means they can be applied rather too easily. They can be applied without any need for justification. It is only if the labels are challenged that justification may be demanded. The immense ease of this sort of judgement makes thinking unnecessary and the outcomes very poor. The applied judgements are just as easily based on emotions as on logic.

━━━━━●━━━━━━●━━━━━

A one-legged cyclist goes in to register for a marathon cycle race in Cape Town. As he is coming out other cyclists going in ask what the one-legged person is doing. He replies that he is registering for the cycle race. The two-legged cyclists protest that this is unfair: 'You have only one leg to get tired but the rest of us have two legs to get tired.' This little story is perfectly logical but illustrates how important perception is in thinking. You can look at a tiny part of the situation and make a logical comment. In the broad picture, however, the comment is no longer valid.

━━━━━●━━━━━━●━━━━━

If you are doing something well, how can that be a bad thing? Complacency is usually the biggest barrier to progress. We can seek to solve problems. We can seek to improve things that are inadequate. We can seek to put right defects. But what do you do if things are working well? Our traditional orientation towards problems, defects and faults means that we do not seek to change or challenge things that are going well. Yet an adequate way of doing something may be very far from the best.

I have always shaved with a wet razor. I started off using a shaving brush and a dish of shaving soap. Then I moved on to shaving foam in a can. As I travel a lot, someone suggested that there was no need to carry with me a can of shaving soap, since ordinary soap was just as good. So I switched to ordinary soap and used it for many years. At Christmas, recently, my cracker gave me a simple shaving brush. So I tried it and liked it. I bought a good-quality brush and now use this with ordinary soap. Shaving is very much better than before. To use a shaving brush you do not need shaving soap. There are two interesting points here. The first is the initial association between a shaving brush and special shaving soap. Somehow it was assumed that a shaving brush would only work with shaving soap. Then there was the complacency factor. I was not seeking a better way of shaving. If the Christmas cracker had not delivered a shaving brush I would never have moved on to using one.

When I travel I often run out of business cards because I meet a lot of people at seminars and other occasions. I could carry a lot with me or I could seek to have them printed at my destination. Printing at the destination might be difficult and take time. So I now have a film which contains photographs of my address, web site, etc. All I need to do is to take this film to any photographic shop and have it developed in an hour or so. I then cut up the

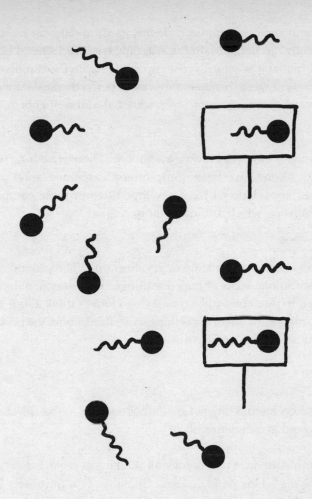

Discrimination

The toles are happily swimming about. Then someone notices that some toles have two 'waves' in their tails and some have three. So two distinct labels are set up – based on physical characteristics. Now there can be discrimination into two types of tole.

prints and have one hundred and fifty cards of different sizes. The idea is obvious in hindsight but was only triggered when I bought a camera that was good for close-up work. Again the complacency factor was at work. Business cards were perfectly satisfactory and the way of obtaining them was traditional and well known.

●━━━━━●

The tying of men's ties is very traditional. There is nothing wrong with it. There have been some minor variations, such as the Windsor knot. Lately I have developed two or three completely different ways which are much more elegant.

●━━━━━●

Matters reach a steady state or equilibrium. There are no actual faults so no one seeks to improve things. They stay like that. We get used to them being like that. We no longer think about them. You cannot think about everything so we think about the problems that do need thinking about.

(Written on the balcony at Le Northolme hotel in the Seychelles, looking out at Silhouette island)

In North American psychology all thinking is regarded as 'problem-solving'. This simply means 'thinking for a purpose'. There is something we want to achieve. Such thinking is different from reflection or reminiscing. At the same time this choice of the word 'problem' is very unfortunate. In general use, problem means that there is a difficulty, a deviation from what should be. A problem means that something is wrong and we want to put it right. Since the major trend of Western thinking habits is already towards 'fault correction', this use of the word 'problem' only reinforces that tendency. The result is to suggest that all thinking is problem-solving; that all thinking is concerned with putting right what is wrong. This leaves out the huge and important areas of constructive thinking, creative thinking and design thinking. This is thinking concerned not with putting right faults but with creating new things. The concern with problems also reinforces complacency. If something is 'not a problem' in the usual lay sense of the word, then there is no point in thinking about it. So the adequate continues, because it is 'not a problem'.

●━━━━━●

The human brain is a wonderful mechanism in which nerve networks allow incoming information to organize itself into patterns. These patterns form the routine response to the world outside. The excellence of the brain is that it learns to cope with a stable environment. The brain finds it very much more difficult to cope with a changing environment and even more difficult to set out to change the environment. So conservatism and complacency are very much the natural state of the brain.

How would a wine connoisseur react to a totally new wine. She would savour it and talk of resemblances to known wine. The new wine might be analysed in terms of standard taste definitions: flinty, raspberry, flowery, oaked, etc. Without such comparison judgements all the connoisseur would be able to say would be: 'I like it' or 'I don't like it.' The past gives reality and richness to the present. The judgement habits of the last millennium make such comparisons possible and useful. The design habits of the next millennium may design tastes that can still be described in past terms – but may also design tastes that need getting to know, and require a new vocabulary.

5

Logic does not change emotions, but if perception changes then emotions change.

If 90 per cent of the errors in ordinary thinking are errors of perception, what can we do about perception? It is astonishing that in the last two thousand years education has done virtually nothing about perception. It is true that education tries to fill our minds with experiences from literature, etc., to enrich our perceptions. All this is pretty useless if we do not have a framework for taking charge of our perceptions. An explorer returns from a newly discovered island and reports that there is a smoking volcano and a bird which does not fly. These are the things that caught his attention. The sponsors of the exploration are not satisfied. So they send the explorer back with a full set of instructions as to where to direct his attention. He is to go to the centre of the island and then look north and note what he sees; then east; then south; then west. He is to look in a 'direction' and put down whatever is to be seen in that direction. He is also instructed to look at the plants, the bird life, soil, etc. These are all directions of 'looking'. In general we have not provided our students with 'directions' of looking. The Cort Thinking Lessons programme does exactly this. The effect has proved to be very powerful.

Two hundred and fifty top women executives were asked to consider the proposition that women be paid 15 per cent more than men for doing the same job; 85 per cent of those present thought it was a good idea, 'and about time too!' Then they were all given a simple 'attention-directing tool' from the Cort

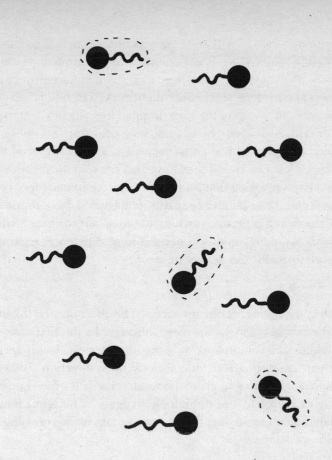

Different and Wrong

If everyone is going in the same direction, then anyone who is going in a different direction is 'wrong'. The other direction might be better – but it is still wrong.

programme, the C&S (Consequences and Sequel). The thinker is formally required to direct attention to the immediate consequences, the short-term consequences, the medium-term consequences and the long-term consequences. As a result of doing this the number in favour of the idea dropped from 85 per cent to just 10 per cent. Now each one of these senior executives would have claimed always to look at consequences as a normal part of their thinking. How else would they have become senior executives? It is therefore surprising that a simple attention-directing tool could make such a huge difference. Over and again, I have found this to be the case. Simple and obvious attention-directing tools which everyone would claim to use make a huge difference when they are used formally and deliberately.

●━━━━━━━●

'Look at the ceiling.' 'Look upwards.' The effect may be the same but the two instructions are very different. In the first case you are asking someone to look at something specific. In the second case you are asking someone to look in a 'direction'. When a youngster is learning to cross the road in the UK, the youngster is taught: 'Look left, look right, look left again.' This is much more valuable than just saying: 'Look out for cars before crossing the road.'

●━━━━━━━●

So when youngsters are taught to 'to do an OPV', they deliberately direct their attention to the views of other people involved in the situation. They attempt to 'look' in that direction and note what they see. Many a conflict has simply dissolved when the combatants have done an OPV on each other.

●━━━━━━━●

During and after the Dark Ages in Europe the Church dominated learning, scholarship, thinking and the universities. At its higher levels, the thinking of the Church was much concerned with heresies and working out the divine will. For all this thinking, certain starting concepts were provided and accepted: for example, that God existed outside of time. Since the starting perceptions were given, the thinking was much concerned with the logical deductions that could be derived from these concepts and perceptions. So the emphasis in thinking was very much on logic and not much on perception. Logic also seemed attractive because the thinker seemed to move from the certain to a new certainty. Perception was much less certain because there could be different perceptions. Which one was right?

Logic does not change emotions but if perception changes, then emotions change. A novelist once suggested that a wife could tell if her husband was seeing another woman during the day by noticing the difference in the length of his tie on his leaving in the morning and on returning in the evening. So one day a husband returns and his wife notes that his tie is a very different length from what it was when he left in the morning. She is very upset and accuses him of having a mistress. He explains that he has been playing squash! Once the perception has changed then the emotions also change. The man might still have a girlfriend but the tie test is now meaningless. Very often people are upset because someone seems to have done something to slight them. A simple explanation of the underlying reasons for the behaviour can change the emotions immediately. You cannot often argue people out of emotions but you can provide alternative perceptual possibilities.

Perception and wisdom are closely allied. Cleverness is a sharp-focus camera. Wisdom is a wide-angle lens. Many clever people are not wise. Many people who are not specially clever in the conventional sense are wise. Wisdom can come with age and experience so you learn to recognize complex possibilities. Wisdom can also be obtained at an earlier age by learning to broaden and enrich perception. You need to look widely. You need to look at alternative possibilities (enrich). You need to look more deeply – into the future. All these aspects of perception feed directly into wisdom.

●━━━━━●

One of the main purposes of judgement is prediction. Once the doctor has diagnosed influenza, then the natural course of that illness, and the possible complications, can be predicted and expected. If you know that something is made of wax you know it will melt when heated. Chemists spend their time identifying substances so they can predict behaviour. If you judge someone to be untrustworthy, then you will expect untrustworthy behaviour from that person. All actions have their effect in the future. Every next minute of our lives is a more or less unpredictable future. So judgement is of a high value in telling us what might happen and what will happen. If our judgement is mistaken or too simplistic, our actions will be inappropriate. In general, judgement is our way of making sense of the world. Once we have done this then we can find our way around that world more easily.

●━━━━━●

We seek to solve problems by identifying the cause and then seeking to remove that cause. That seems obvious. If the problem is caused by 'something', then remove that something and the problem is automatically removed at the same time. In practice it is not quite so simple. It may not be easy to isolate the cause. There may be many possible causes. You may find the cause but be unable to remove it. You may find that the cause is 'human nature' and you are unlikely to change that. In all such cases we become paralysed because we cannot proceed in the usual problem-solving way. Most of the world's major problems will not be solved by further analysis. The problems have been analysed enough already. What we need to do is to 'design a way forward', leaving the cause in place.

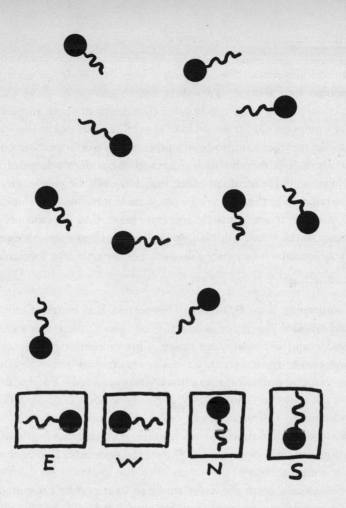

E   W   N   S

Analysis

The toles are swimming in all directions. Someone decides that this haphazard movement can be analysed into four broad directions: north, south, east and west. All movement can now be analysed in terms of these directions – even if the fit is not exact.

In the Philippines they had built a huge hall to house an international film festival. Two days before the event there was a typhoon and the hall was flooded to a depth of about three feet. The engineers said it would take several days to pump the water out. So they got hundreds of workmen to build a platform over the water. The meeting took place with the water underneath the delegates. This sort of approach may too easily be condemned as 'papering over the cracks'. In some instances this would indeed be the case and is not to be recommended; find the cause of the cracks or the house may fall down. In other instances, designing a way forward is not only valuable, it is the only way forward.

If something is good, then surely more of it is better? Once we have applied the judgement value of 'good', then that thing is good – and we want good things. Once something is placed in the 'good-to-have' box then we want more and more. Yet there are so many instances where this is simply not true. Food without any salt tastes bad. Some salt is good. Too much salt is again bad. I sometimes call this the salt curve. No communication is bad. More communication is good. Surely, more and more communication can only be better? The average American manager gets 178 e-mail messages every day. Because e-mail is so easy, you automatically send the same message to everyone on your list. It is possible to be overwhelmed and burdened by too much communication. Free movement of money and goods is the opposite of protectionism and is good for trade. But the unrestricted adoration of 'globalism' may not be an unmixed blessing. Money surges around the world in search of immediate gain and at the expense of sustained productivity. Water in a basin flops about. Put a grid in the basin and the giant flops are reduced to tiny flops in each square of the grid. Freedom is good and more and more freedom is better. But at a certain point freedom becomes licence

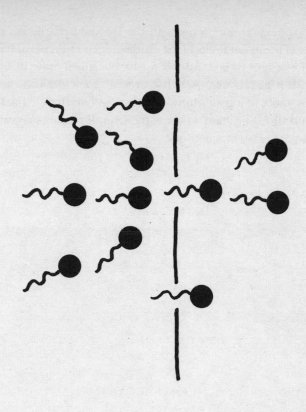

Possibilities

The toles are streaming through the centre hole, which is the obvious and established route. Two toles have discovered alternative possibilities. To find these you have to think of 'possibilities'.

51

and your freedom interferes with the freedom of others. This is another of the major faults of the crude judgement system. It is easy to acknowledge this fault intellectually, but much more difficult to deal with it in practice. At what precise point does the striving towards 'more of a good thing' turn into a 'bad thing'? Each next step must surely be good – even if the overall picture suggests that the ultimate effect is not good?

The brain is designed to learn through repeated exposure. Gradually patterns are formed. These patterns are then used on future occasions. The choice of the appropriate pattern depends on judgement. The brain has a very discriminating flip-flop system. The activated nerves flip into A or flop into B state. There is no in-between. In fact the brain does very much what Aristotle wanted it to do: make sharp and firm judgements. There is no natural mechanism in the brain for creative thinking, constructive thinking or design thinking. We want to know 'what is' so that we can respond with a tried and known routine pattern.

6

So universities found it
useful to look backwards
and scholarship
attained a high value.
Unfortunately most
universities have never
recovered from that
idiom.

(Looking out over a beach at Le Northolme hotel at Beauvallon in the Seychelles; palm trees, rocks, beach and surf)

Call centres are becoming big business. There is an estimate in the European Union that soon 1 per cent of the working population will be employed in call centres. These centres consist of dozens of people sitting at desks and telephones. They answer complaints and inquiries from the public. The call centres deal with many different organizations. In effect these organizations have 'outsourced' their public communication operations to the call centres. You can imagine a call-centre operator having a list of twenty-three standard types of complaint. In the first few seconds of the conversation the operator will seek to place the caller into one of the standard types of caller. Then there is a standard way of dealing with that caller. The standard responses may not apply to the whole caller but only to specified situations. Whether such lists are overt and formal, or only within the minds of individual operators, does not matter. In either case, being able to recognize a standard situation allows a standard response. This is much easier than having to figure out a response each time. It is hardly surprising that this fundamental approach with its huge advantages has become the dominant habit of human thinking.

●━━━━●

An architect is sitting in his or her office and a client comes in who wants a house built. The architect does not pull out of the desk drawer a book of *101 Designs for a House*. The architect does not suggest the client has the house in page 71. If this was the procedure, there would be no need for an architect. The contractor could have the book or the client could buy the book directly. It is true that the architect could have some value, advising the client which standard house to choose. The purpose of the architect is, usually, not so much judgement as design. The architect sets out to design a house that fits the client's needs, desires and budget. The house must also fit the environment and comply with regulations. The architect does not have to design everything from scratch: roof materials, bathroom fittings, floor tiles, etc. The architect makes full use of standard elements – and exercises judgement in the choice of available standard elements. Yet the design is a design. Music makes use of standard notes yet each piece of music is an original design. Design is a matter of putting together what we know in order to achieve what we want.

•————————•

In some cases design may consist of 'modifying' a standard response to suit a particular need better. So a dressmaker may modify a standard pattern to fit a figure that is slightly more full than usual. A standard contract may be modified to fit a particular fear. A judge has to deliver standard sentences but may modify them somewhat; a judge is not supposed to design new and imaginative sentences.

•————————•

It is said that all the standard stories have been told. Any new story is simply a variation of the standard story. This may be true if we set the concepts broadly enough: 'boy loves girl, trouble, but it works out in the end'. Similarities at a very broad concept level do not mean much. A horse is the same as an aeroplane – because both of them are 'ways of getting from A to B'. This comparison is not of much practical value. Broad concepts are very useful in thinking – but if they are to be put into practice, they need to be brought down to specific ideas.

•————————•

In some ways 'design' is the opposite of analysis. In analysis we break things down into standard and recognizable parts. In design we put things together to achieve a value and a purpose. In some ways design is the opposite of judgement. In judgement we seek to find a standard response for a standard situation. In design we seek to put together a new response that fits the situation better.

•——————•

It is unfortunate that the word 'creativity' has been pre-empted by the arts world – and that the word 'design' has been pre-empted in much the same way: 'graphic design', 'architectural design', 'clothes design', etc. These areas are genuinely design-oriented, but the danger is that design may be seen as 'non-essential'. After all, clothes will protect and keep you warm even if they are not the latest Paris (or Milan) fashion. A house will serve its purpose even if it is the same standard shape as it has been for hundreds of years. Design may be seen as having an 'added value'; an aesthetic value; a commercial value; and a fashion value. The suggestion is that you could do it anyway but it would be 'better' if it was well designed. There was even a period when designers went crazy and insisted that everything had to look 'designed', even if this added nothing at all in value. It is this 'superfluous' aspect of design that is unfortunate. There are times when there is no way forward at all. There is a need to design a way forward. There was no standard way of getting to the moon. A way had to be designed. Surgeons often design new operations: like treating spina bifida in the womb.

•——————•

At the time of the Renaissance universities found they could learn much more by looking backwards at the learning and wisdom of the Greek–Roman period than by trying to look forward. Scholarship was very important. Finding out what others had thought through was a good way of developing new ideas – and practical. So universities found it useful to look backwards and scholarship attained a high value. Unfortunately most universities have never recovered from that idiom. They are still mainly

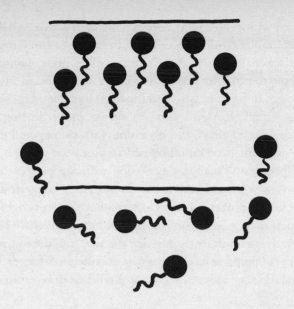

Positive and Constructive Thinking

In the top part the toles are adjusting to the block and thinking 'positive' thoughts about their situation. This is positive thinking. In the bottom part the toles are finding a way around the block. This is constructive thinking.

concerned with scholarship and looking backwards. A scholarly work has to refer to all the work that has gone before – otherwise it is not taken seriously. An eminent Nobel prize winner once advised me to put long lists of references at the end of my books even though these were false and the ideas had been my own: that way they would be taken more seriously in the 'academic' game. This arises directly from the obsession with history and the past in the Renaissance, when scholarship was indeed the best way of making progress. This huge obsession with the past crowds out something which is at least equally important: a concern with the future. Outside obvious courses like architecture and engineering, how much time is spent on 'design' in most university courses? How can the best minds help design the way into the future when this aspect of thinking has been given so little importance? At least one third of every university course should be devoted to design.

•———————•

Hypotheses need to be designed. Scientists are too often taught that science is the collection of data, the analysis of data and the logical deduction of principles. I have had appointments at the universities of Oxford, Cambridge, Harvard and London, and I have seen this happening. It is total rubbish. Without hypotheses science cannot advance. Two thousand years ago Chinese science and technology was way ahead of the West. And they are very smart people indeed. So what happened? The technicians were making progress. Then it got into the hands of the mandarin class (and scholars) who described everything as it was. They never invented the hypothesis: that key piece of mental software. So progress came to an abrupt halt. A hypothesis is a 'designed' possibility. It cannot be designed by logic or judgement. There is a need for creative imagination. Though they may indeed exist, I have never seen a substantial course on 'hypothesis' design in a university. The dominance of the 'analysis' frame of mind in universities is to blame.

•———————•

'Data mining' with computers suggests the detailed analysis of data to pick out trends and correlations. For example, analysis of the sales from a supermarket may show that when there is a high sale of children's toys there is also a high sale of whisky. This may suggest that fathers are taking their children shopping. If this happens on a particular day, special attractions for fathers might be scheduled for that day. A lot of useful information may be obtained in this way. The danger is that such forms of analysis may be seen to be sufficient. They are not. Data mining will only reveal a small fraction of the information available. It is only when hypotheses are 'designed' that the full value of the data will be revealed. When I was doing research on blood flow through the lungs the data did not fit standard flow considerations (pressure differential, resistance, flow, etc.). It was only when I put in the 'possibility' that it was not a tube but a 'waterfall' that it made any sense. The height of a waterfall has no effect on the flow over the fall. The immense value of constructs and hypotheses is too easily forgotten in the days of the superb analytical capabilities of computers. Once again there is the need to supplement analytical thinking with design thinking. It is not a matter of one or the other. Both are needed. Historically the pendulum has swung very far towards analysis and this needs to be corrected.

If something is fine, excellent and effective, then why should you not use it? Our judgement and analysis system is fine, excellent and effective. So why do I seem to be attacking it? The answer is that I am not 'attacking' it at all. It is our dialectic system which suggests that if I am not happy with something, then I must be 'attacking it'. I think it is an excellent system and it would be absurd to attack it. But it may not be enough. The front left wheel of a motor car is excellent and I would not dream of attacking the value of the front left wheel of a motor car. That would be absurd. But I can point out that the front left wheel, however excellent, is not enough. Our traditional thinking is excellent – but not enough.

There is a cook who cooks the world's best omelette. This omelette is served for breakfast, for lunch and for dinner, day after day. The omelette is still excellent. The cook is still excellent. But the omelette is not enough. Our usual dialectic system insists that something is either good or bad. How can something be both good and bad at the same time? Well, it can be very good but bad at the same time if we regard it as sufficient – or if it crowds out anything else. Our traditional thinking system is indeed excellent but also bad if it leads people to believe that this system is sufficient by itself. The very excellence of the system for some purposes has led too many people to believe in its sufficiency.

Our traditional system of thinking is very good at defending itself because it picks the rules of the game, the concepts and the values. 'Truth' is seen as all-important. But what about 'values', 'productivity' and 'creativity'. Our existing systems do indeed contribute in these areas, but not sufficiently. The idioms of creative thinking and design thinking are much more powerful. Unfortunately, those who espouse such values are not usually very good at expressing them in the thought-language required by the traditionalists.

Style

There is no one 'right' style. Things that are different may each be an excellent example of a different style. Three types of tole are shown. Each is true to its style.

Why do some people read horoscopes? Possibly because they want 'someone' to tell them what is going to happen. What about 'designing' what is going to happen? If you have been taught to recognize standard situations and to respond with the standard response, then the habit of designing the future is never developed. The judgement mode of the last millennium has crowded out the motivation and methods of design.

7

Countless people were burned or drowned as witches because this was the plausible explanation of epilepsy, ergot poisoning and other causes of unusual behaviour.

How can you argue with truth? Surely un-truth is a terrible thing and leads to injustice, ineffectiveness and all manner of trouble. If un-truth is so unworkable, then surely 'truth' has a supreme value? Truth shows us the world around us as it really is. This plant is poisonous: if there is no truth, then you may eat the plant and die. The engineer must trust the truth of his or her mathematics and the material strengths reported by the suppliers. Without truth at every stage the bridge would soon collapse. Almost all religions promote truth as their driving value. With truth humankind can walk along the path of righteousness. To challenge the all-embracing sufficiency of truth is sheer cheek. Such a challenge seems to suggest a championing of un-truth, which would be ridiculous. But to challenge our treatment of truth is not to recommend un-truth but to explore that treatment. What are the dangers? What are the limitations? What are the deficiencies? Does the banner of 'truth' lead to much harm?

●————————●

Any challenge to the supremacy of truth can easily be met by the claim that any fault arising from 'truth' really arises from 'false truth'. This is understandable and acceptable in a pure sense. We can, however, deal with practical life, with the way the 'truth' concept is understood, used and abused. No matter how ideal a concept is in its 'pure state', if the practical and 'impure' use of that concept has dangers, then those dangers need to be pointed out. One of the more obvious dangers of 'truth' is arrogance. If you believe that you have the 'truth', then you may exercise the right to oppress others who think differently. Religious wars and persecutions have arisen from such arrogance. The ways in which this feeling of truth have been arrived at vary with different religions. Then there is the arrogance that arises from a fixed set of perceptions. If you look at something one way, then you can arrive at a truth consistent with those perceptions. It may not occur to you that there may be other perceptions of equal validity. The cohesion of a logical argument says nothing about the validity of the starting perceptions. Because of our traditional emphasis on logic and our dismissal of perception we often overlook this dangerous cause of arrogance.

●————————●

There are many types of truth – which, of course, we treat as 'one truth'. There is 'game truth'. This means that if we set up a certain 'game', then truths arise within that game. If we set up a number system, as in mathematics, then operating the rules of that system will result in certain 'truths'. If you start with certain shapes, then the way those shapes fit together will be a 'truth' – other ways would not work. If you start with certain concepts and perceptions, then the way these fit together will also be a truth consistent with the starting-points. There was a very famous philosopher with whom I used to have occasional conversations. In the end it became rather boring because it was a matter of logical manipulation of fixed starting concepts – there was no exploration or development. While it has its validity, this sort of logical sequence tends to be rather sterile. If you play poker or bridge, there are certain things you are allowed to do and others you are not allowed to do (like signalling to your partner at bridge). These are the 'truths' of that game. If you draw a right-angled triangle, then the square of the hypotenuse is equal to the sum of the squares on the other sides. This was discovered by Pythagoras about 2,600 years ago. It is an inevitable consequence of drawing a right-angled triangle on a plane surface. If you set things up in a certain way, then a certain consequence is inevitable – we treat this as a truth. If we were not playing that game, then the truth would not be there

●———————●

Experience truth means that in our experience something is so. You may be certain that the grocery shop is on the right-hand side of the road as you enter the village. This has been your experience. You can check out this 'truth' whenever you like. There is nothing 'inevitable' about the shop being there (as there would be in game truth). The shop just happens to be there. Any other person can also check it out. The validity of truth based on your personal experience may not be high. Your memory might be faulty. You might have been deluded, etc. But if lots of other people confirm and re-confirm that truth then we are inclined to treat it as a truth. Even then, lots of people may have been deluded. So scientific proof requires that something can be tested, and retested, in a scientific way. A great number of people believe that if you are constipated you are bad-tempered – but I am not aware of any scientific study to support this widely held 'truth'. A lot of people believe in astrology – but again there is no scientific proof that being born under a particular star sign affects your personality. The same personality profile (based on one star sign) was given to sixty-seven executives. They all claimed that it fitted each of them very well. Yet they had differing birth dates. The whole purpose of science is to try to separate myth, folklore and generally held beliefs from truths which can be proved over and again. Science has done a moderately good job. The reason I use the word 'moderately' is that the interpretation of the data and the theories arising from it are themselves only constructs. The data may indeed be true but the interpretation may not be. We may think it is the only possible interpretation of the data, but then 'proof is often no more than lack of imagination'. If we cannot conceive of another explanation, then we feel the interpretation we have must be true. Over and over again the certainty of the 'truth' has arisen from a poor imagination. If lawyers were ever

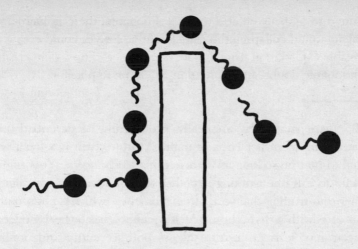

Complacency

There is a way around the obstacle. It works. It is satisfactory.
Everyone uses it. There is, however, a shorter way around which will
never be found if everyone is complacent.

trained to be truly creative (which is possible) the criminal legal system would collapse at once. A creative lawyer could create a possible explanation from any set of evidence. This would create 'reasonable doubt' and conviction would be impossible.

●———————●

All experience 'truths' are really 'proto-truths'. I described this concept in an earlier book of mine. A proto-truth is a truth we hold to be true so long as we are trying to change it. You might prefer to call it a 'working hypothesis'. The advantage of calling it a 'proto-truth' is that we do treat it as true – which is not usually the case with a hypothesis. Action cannot easily be based on uncertainty so a proto-truth allows both certainty and doubt. There is certainty in a practical sense, but not in the absolute sense of unchangeability. If you go to a modest restaurant you can eat the food with enjoyment but you do not believe it is the best food you could possibly have.

●———————●

The third type of truth is 'belief truth'. Paradoxically, this is often held most strongly even though the basis for it is the weakest of all the truths. Belief truth means you have a certain belief. This belief may arise from your experience, from the experience of others or from the teaching of others. This belief now affects your perception. If you believe that people with close-set eyes are shifty and dishonest, then you will see them as such. You will notice and exaggerate any behaviour that reinforces your perception and ignore behaviour that is contrary to your belief. So you will really perceive such people as dishonest and shifty. Your belief truth is confirmed and strengthened. This is the behaviour of stereotypes, prejudices, discriminations, persecutions, etc. Watching a plane making a vapour trail in the sky one farmer says to another: 'They are trying to make rain, you know.' The other farmer asks why he thinks this. To which the first replies: 'You never see them on rainy days, do you now?' Belief truth and scientific theory are not too far apart. A theory will force us to look at things in a way which reinforces that theory. This is particularly true in psychology. Freud's theories and even Darwin's theory of evolution are only belief truths. In its acute form paranoia is an intensification of meaning. Most mental illnesses are a breakdown of some sort or a failure of coordination, but in paranoia there is an excess of coordination, an excess of significance, an excess of meaning. There is an elaborate and rational explanation of why a car parked at a certain spot in the road at a certain time is part of a planned cycle of events. Our justifying and rationalizing abilities are truly superb. That is how we survive and prosper. Belief truth is what propels us forward from day to day. Suppose a psychological theory holds that all daughters love their fathers. If a girl protests that she does not, then this is interpreted as a love so strong that it has to be denied and suppressed. If the girl says she actually hates her father, then that means that a strong love has been thwarted and the same emotion is now expressed in a different form. Whatever the actual situation the belief system interprets it to support that belief system.

●━━━━━●

In addition to all the other dangers that arise from the blinkered adoration of the 'truth', there is the considerable danger that it brings thinking to an end. Once we have arrived at the 'truth' then we can stop thinking. What is the point in thinking further? Once we have arrived at a conclusion or interpretation, then we stop thinking. Truth gives a certain 'closure' to our thinking. The circle has been completed. We grasp at the first plausible explanation. Countless people were burned or drowned as witches because witchcraft was the plausible explanation of epilepsy, ergot poisoning and many other causes of unusual behaviour. When Europe ate rye bread the contaminating ergot fungus caused miscarriages and abortions – and also hallucinations. When the diet switched to wheat bread the population exploded and there were far fewer saints.

All truth has a 'circular' basis. We believe it to be true and perception shows it to be true. We expect it to be true and experience confirms the expectation. We set up the game and find the outcome is predetermined by our set-up.

If we sought to put 'value' instead of 'truth' at the centre of our thinking, we would run into the danger of expediency and opportunism. Ironically, it is the long time span of 'truth' that is both its greatest virtue and also its greatest vice. The long time span creates principles which override expediency and opportunism. At the same time, this long time span gives rigidity and inflexibility, and makes change difficult. Today's supportive truth is tomorrow's restrictive truth.

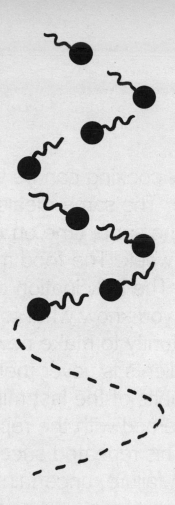

Prediction

The toles seem to be involved in a follow-my-leader zigzag dance.
From this past behaviour it is reasonable to predict future behaviour.

Institutional cooking can be very predictable. The same meals can be served at the same time on the same day of the week. The food may be very good. The anticipation can be enjoyable: you know what to expect. The opportunity to make new use of new ingredients is never there. The thinking habits of the last millennium were concerned with the repetition of success. This repeated success was better than failure, uncertainty or the wastefulness of trial and error. But the new opportunities brought about by new technology, new values and new lifestyles cannot be utilized by mere repetition – no matter how successful.

8

In order to see a new idea there is a need to create it first in the brain as a possibility, a speculation, an hypothesis or a construct.

Some cultures, particularly the North American culture, are very impatient with concepts. North America was a pioneering culture and in a pioneering culture action is always more important than further thinking. Instead of sitting at home and tangling oneself into knots with contemplative thinking, it was more useful to go out and claim more land, drill another oil well, kill a few more Indians, extend the railway, etc. Concepts are regarded as effete academic exercises that produce nothing. Direct hands-on action is more important. 'Don't tell me what to think – tell me what to do tomorrow.' In an expanding universe there is a lot to be said for this action orientation. (It applied in the British Empire too.) Simple actions repeated with conviction and effectiveness were indeed rewarding. But when the expansion is over, then another sort of thinking is required. This is the thinking involved in rearranging things to get more value out of what is already available. This is design thinking and redesign thinking. Energy that is locked up in existing structures can be released to energize new structures. Expansion thinking needs an unchanging base. When expansion stops value will only come from design thinking.

●━━━━━━●

You drive to a beach but when you get there it is crowded and smelly. Music is being played too loudly. Rather unattractive people are playing volleyball all over the place. You try to find your way down the beach to a quieter spot. It is not easy because there is no road along the beach. It would make more sense to

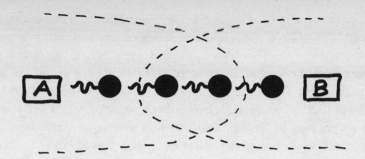

Perception

One perception (dotted line) sees the toles as fleeing from A. Another perception sees the toles as seeking out B. Perception is the way we look at things.

drive back to the nearest junction (or roundabout) and take another road to the beach. Concepts are junctions in the mind. It is not easy to move from an idea to another idea. It is easier to move back from the idea to the concept and then from the concept to another idea. If you meet a child you cannot easily discover that child's brothers and sisters. So you seek out the parents and then it is very easy to find the brothers and sisters. Concepts have a key role to play in design thinking. Once you identify a value concept then you seek out the different ways of delivering that value.

It is said that NASA had a problem with ballpoint pens because they did not write upside down. Such pens depend on gravity to feed the ink on to the ball. So the pens did not work in the zero-gravity environment of space. A considerable amount of money was put into developing a 'space pen', in which a pressure system forced the ink on to the ball. This worked very well. It is said that the Russian space programme had the same problem but went to the concept: 'We need something that writes upside down.' So they used a pencil.

In all creative and design thinking 'concepts' play a key role. There is a need to design concepts. There is a need to generate alternative concepts. There is a need to move across concept levels from broad to specific and back again. There is a need to create ways of implementing the concept through specific and practical ideas. All these aspects are largely, but not entirely, absent from thinking based on analysis, judgement and the use of standard responses.

There are those who believe that the analysis of data will produce new ideas. This is extremely unlikely, since the brain can only see what it is prepared to see. The existing brain patterns (and their catchment area) will ensure that the data are seen in terms of existing ideas. In order to see a new idea there is a need to create it first in the brain as a possibility, a speculation, an hypothesis or a construct. This needs creativity, design and imagination. You cannot create a new dish just by analysing past successful dishes. You need to dream up 'possibilities' and then try them out. Have you tried a mixture of Marmite (Vegemite in Australia) and marmalade? Did you know that Pernod is very good in pumpkin soup and whisky in chicken soup? Gin or Sambuco in tomato soup is reasonably well known. The strategy of 'speculate and try' is as essential for data analysis as it is for design. The 'trying out' may be only a thought experiment or a real mini experiment or a computer simulation or a mess in the kitchen.

A dictionary tells us to spell a word the way it should be spelled. If it were not so, communication would be in chaos. So how do we design the new words that are so badly needed if we are to change perceptions? We may say that if there is a real need for the word, then that word will evolve. This is true, but what about those new words which we should be creating ahead of need. The new word will make us look at things in a different way. The new word needs to come first and then experience will follow. The new word needs to be 'designed'. Such a word does not reflect reality but creates reality. The judgement system of the last millennium is based on reflecting past reality and has no energy for designing new realities.

9

You may discover the
truth but you need to
design value.

We forget just how powerful perception can be. At a high-tech meeting there were about fifteen hundred computer scientists and other technical wizards. At the end of the meeting someone was to draw a number from a bag. If this number matched the number on your registration badge you would win some marvellous computer set-up. The person organizing the draw took a number, looked at it and then threw it away. He proceeded to draw another number. Almost everyone in the room got very upset at this. Why? They perceived that the number thrown away might indeed have been their number. Why? There is just as much chance of the next number to be drawn being 'your number' as the first one. You might well benefit from the first number being thrown away. The difficulty is that our perception fixes on the number being thrown away but not on 'the next number'. Of course, it could be said that people were upset at the 'unfairness' of the procedure, which departed from the normal, expected procedure.

●————————●

People are upset with concepts because they are vague and intangible. How do you know you have the right concept? Then there are several levels of concepts: from the very broad to the more specific to the specific. Which level should you be at? We want to motivate the salespeople. We want to give incentives to the salespeople. We should give a monetary reward to the salespeople. These are all different concept levels. At the end there might be specific ideas such as increasing the sales commission; having awards for the best-performing salespeople; setting targets and

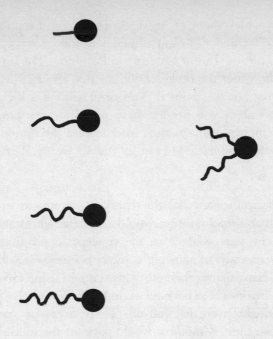

Evolution

The left side of the page shows a possible evolution of a tole. The tail gets longer and longer and may provide better survival value. The right side of the page shows the 'design' of a double tail. Evolution is slow and does not provide big jumps. Design is faster and can be more radical.

rewarding achievement; giving stock options, etc. I want a holiday in the Mediterranean. I want a holiday in Italy. I want a holiday in Italy by the sea. I want a holiday in Portofino. The broader the concept the wider the range of options that spring from it – but the less you can do about it. You cannot book a flight 'to the Mediterranean' – you need to have a specific destination. The more specific the concept the more narrow the options. If you choose 'Italy', you exclude France, Malta, Greece, Tunisia, etc.

If you said that the concept behind parking meters was 'to organize parking' that broad concept would not generate many specific ideas. If you narrowed down the concept to say that parking meters 'were a way of allowing as many people as possible to use limited parking space', then other ideas might come forward. For example, anyone could park as long as he or she wished – provided their headlights were left full on. There is now a 'downward pressure' on time. A motorist would park for the minimum time otherwise the battery would be run flat. This might be useful in a shopping area where only a few minutes' parking time was needed. Or some spaces might be used this way while others had traditional meters.

There are two hawks. Hawk A has superb eyesight. From a great height this hawk can recognize a frog. This hawk lives on frogs and evolves to be interested only in frogs. Then there is hawk B with very poor eyesight. Because its eyesight is so poor this hawk has to form a general concept: small things that move might be good to eat. So whenever hawk B sees a small thing moving it swoops. It feeds on frogs, mice, lizards and big insects. Some things it spits out. Obviously, hawk A with its superb eyesight is superior to hawk B. Not so. If frogs die out then hawk A also dies out. Its diet is too specific. If frogs die out hawk B is not much affected because there are many other 'small-things-that-move'. Because hawk B has a concept that hawk has flexibility. Without concepts there is no flexibility.

●━━━●

Once you have identified the concept you can modify it, improve it or change it. If you only have a vague idea of the concept you cannot do anything with the 'vague idea'. So it helps to verbalize or spell out the concept. Much of traditional economics is based on the concept of 'exchange'. You exchange work for money. You exchange money for goods or services. This is so fundamental a concept that we may doubt if it could ever be changed. In the animal kingdom economics has a different concept: 'to each according to his ability and power – from each according to his nature'. There is no exchange concept in the animal world. There are many other possible economic concepts, particularly if we consider self-organizing systems. In the future we need to explore and design new economic concepts, as the ones we have are not completely satisfactory for everyone.

●━━━●

In some respects a small wooden toothpick is more valuable than a gold bar. A gold bar only has indirect value. There is not much you could do with it directly except perhaps use it as a doorstop or paperweight, as gold is so heavy. If you are desperate for a toothpick a gold bar is not much use. If you are in a remote place where the conversion facilities are not to hand, then a gold bar is not much use. A gold bar is full of potential value. You can convert it into money. You can borrow money against it as collateral. You can make jewellery from it if you have the equipment and expertise. You can impress everyone around (but invite burglary).

●━━━●

'Benefits' are the interaction between something and the benefici-ary. In practice there is not too much point in distinguishing benefits from values so long as we treat values as dependent. A prestige fountain-pen writes well. A fountain-pen (or other writing instrument) may be needed to take down a crucial telephone number. A pen may be needed to sign an important contract. The pen may be used to prop open a window to get more ventilation. The gift of a prestige pen may show that you appreciate the work someone is doing. Your flashing the pen around may impress others as to your credit-worthiness. A pen may be a choice as a Christmas present when you cannot think of anything else. All these potential values or benefits are inherent in the pen and become real depending on circumstances, need and the person. Some people would avoid a prestige pen because it gives the wrong impression.

Any design process demands a high degree of 'value sensitivity'. Photographic film has an indicator of light sensitivity. A 200 iso film is not very sensitive; a 400 iso film is more sensitive; a 1000 iso film is extremely sensitive to light. Without value sensitivity there is no point in seeking to be creative. I have sat in on creative sessions where excellent ideas have been produced. But those present have been unable to see the value in their own ideas. They were looking for only one value and failed to see the others. So value sensitivity is central to creativity and design. We need to know the values we are aiming for. We need to know the values that emerge even when not sought out.

'Value' is clearly a positive word and means good things and something worth having. What about things that are negative and not worth having? We may not seek these out but they may arise in the course of a design. Suppose an architect designs an impressive building with a wide sweeping staircase leading up to the front door. There are a lot of values here. The staircase, however, makes life hard for wheelchairs, arthritics and older people. This was hardly the intention of the architect but is a 'side-effect' of the

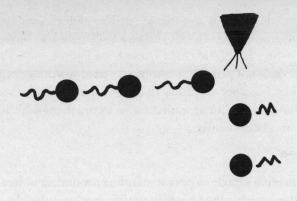

Problem-Solving

The triangular death ray is killing the toles. Traditional problem-solving would seek to remove the cause of the problem. Sometimes we cannot do this and need to 'design' a way around – leaving the cause in place.

magnificent design. We can use words like 'defects', 'faults' and 'disadvantages', but these tend to imply a fault in the way something is done – which is not the case. There is no fault in the staircase. Language does not provide a commonly used word for 'negative values'. So it becomes necessary to use the term 'negative values', even if that is really a contradiction in terms. Language is very deficient in process words.

•——————————•

We can imagine a circle of people standing around an object. The object is the same but the people have different 'agendas'. Suppose the object is a *haute couture* dress at rather a high price. One person thinks it is a ridiculous waste of money. Another person thinks that it is very expensive but she could just afford it – and it is worth it. Someone thinks the cut would not suit her figure at all. Someone else thinks the dress would be perfect for 'making a splash' at the upcoming charity ball. Another person thinks of it as a 'guilt offering' for his wife with whom he is currently quarrelling. Another person thinks the colour is ghastly. Another person swears by the designer name. Another person believes that anyone wearing the dress would look ridiculous and pretentious. Another person believes that wearing the dress shows courage and a devil-may-care attitude. Another person may think of all the work and hype that has gone into high fashion and how this energy might have been more sensibly used. Another person thinks that the 'fun things' in life are important and that deadly seriousness at every moment makes for a very boring life. Another person wonders whether her local dressmaker could make up something similar for less. Another person stands there calculating the profit margin on the dress and the financial mechanics of *haute couture*. A fashion journalist finds the dress exciting to write about. A fashion photographer wonders how best to shoot the dress. Then there is the owner of the salon, wondering whether that dress will sell. The designer is concerned whether the dress will enhance his reputation. A rival designer is slightly jealous and trying to hide this from himself. So there are

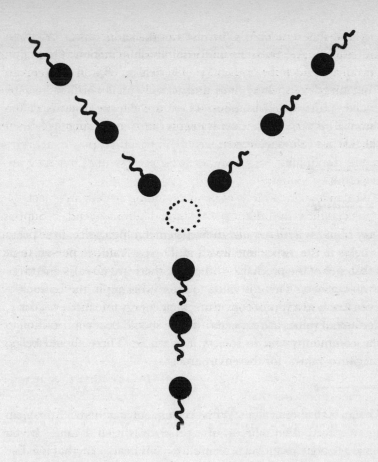

Starting Point

In the centre is the 'truth'. How you get there depends entirely on where you start from.

eighteen different 'values' involved in the same object. All these are relative. Are there no universal absolute values? There are, and these tend to be 'system' values: health, education, freedom from bullying, shelter, food and water, etc., to which may be added spiritual nourishment. These are the basic needs of the 'human system'. Once that system is functioning effectively then the relative values take over: wealth, importance, power, achievement, tranquillity, etc. None of these are essential but they are nevertheless values.

●━━━━━●

Any business is an organization designed to provide value. There is value to the owner and investor. There is value to the buyer or consumer of the products – otherwise there are no sales and there is no business. There is value to those working in the business – even if only as a way of converting their energy into money. Today, additional values are expected. There should be a contribution to the community and to society as a whole. There should be no 'negative values' for the environment.

●━━━━━●

Design is all about values. With problem-solving there is a problem to be solved. The solution of a problem is itself a value. If you have a headache and an aspirin cures your headache, that is value. If you feel seasick and something removes that feeling, that is a very high value. Where it is not a matter of problem-solving, the whole purpose of design is to create value. There is no 'need' for the design as such. The only justification is that new values are provided. A great deal of our thinking is concerned with finding the 'truth' so that we can find our way around. Design thinking is concerned with creating value.

●━━━━━●

Would it be a value if passengers could really sleep on long-distance flights? The passengers might benefit. There would be less demand on food, beverage and cabin attention. The negative value would be the need to reorganize the plane each time the flight direction changed, involving a change to daytime flying. This could actually be overcome if planes only flew eastward as eastward flights tend to be overnight: New York to London; London to Singapore; Singapore to Los Angeles; Los Angeles to New York. So planes equipped with bunks and beds would always fly around the world in one direction.

●━━━━━━●

We spend far too little time thinking about value creation and value design. Our education systems do virtually nothing to develop the habits and skills of value design. Education is all about the past, all about 'what is'. We recognize things and know what to do about them. We identify the correct routine to use. If values existed before, then we are able to reapply the methods which delivered those values. There is nothing about the creation of new values. If values did not exist before then we cannot deliver them. Clearly this sort of thinking is not good enough. Excellent photographs of past buildings do not design new buildings.

●━━━━━━●

At a meeting concerned with the contribution of high technology to education, the technology was brilliant but the education concepts were old-fashioned and feeble. Showing a tired concept with brilliant colour and high definition does not make it a better concept. Technology is far ahead of the value concepts that we ask it to deliver. More and more technology is not the answer. More and more technology will deliver less and less value. Technology companies that pursue only technology will find the delivered value getting less and less. Faster and faster communication means nothing if there is nothing to communicate. Building more roads to ease traffic only results in more traffic to fill the roads. The ease of e-mail means that a lot of things that are not worth communicating are now communicated. I have seen people overburdened by their e-mail commitments. Technology by itself allows value to be delivered but the value concept has to be there first. The big need in the future is not so much for more technology but for the design of new value concepts. Technology will be able to deliver almost any value concept we design. But the value concepts have to be designed directly. It is said that 90 per cent of people in the USA do not use 95 per cent of the features on their video recorders. The technology is there – but the value is not.

●━━━━●

Value can be both discovered and designed. Much work is being done on native plants and folk remedies in order to discover whether there are indeed powerful substances at work in them. Much research is done to discover new drugs in medicine. At the same time there is an effort to 'design' new medicines by putting molecules together in different combinations. It is not a matter of favouring discovery against design, or the other way around. At this point in history it is a matter of putting sufficient emphasis on 'design', since the emphasis has hitherto been so exclusively on discovery. You may discover the truth but you need to design value.

Design often consists of putting together standard, known routines in a new way to deliver a new value. Design skill often lies in mentally breaking down and framing a situation so that a known answer can be given to each stage. It is the assembly of these standard elements that can give the new design.

10

Those organizations that focused on competition did badly, those that focused on value creation did well.

'Simplicity' is a key value. As the world gets ever more complicated, simplicity is going to become ever more important as a value – otherwise we are going to spend so much time in anxious confusion that we will be unable to enjoy all the benefits offered by technology. That is why I wrote a book specifically on the value of 'simplicity'. A machine may offer wonderful value, but if it is too complicated to use that value is valueless. The same applies to procedures, regulations, laws, etc. At my suggestion a brilliant computer programmer, Phil Backman, has been designing an S button for computers. You press this 'Simple' button and the computer goes into simple mode.

●━━━━━━━●

Every country should have a 'National Institute of Simplicity' to act as a reference body in the matter of complexity. This body would look at new laws or regulations and would give a 'reference opinion'. If this opinion suggested that the matter was too complex, then there would be some pressure to simplify it. The institute could also set up task forces to work with people in any field to simplify processes in that field (law, etc.).

●━━━━━━━●

When workers in Europe were asked what they would like most, the answers differed in different countries. In some countries, like the UK, there was a desire for more money. In other countries, like Germany, there was a desire for more leisure time. It is true

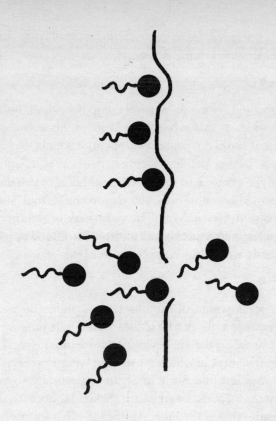

Value Creation

No value is created until it is created. There are attempts to break
through the barrier. Value is only created where there is a real
breakthrough. A design is not a design unless it delivers value.

that this might simply reflect the adequacy of existing wage levels, but it does show that time is becoming an important value.

———•———•———

I once suggested setting up a travel company called 'Boring Holidays'. The idea is that when time is short, an exciting holiday, with lots to see and do, passes before you have noticed it. On the contrary, a 'boring holiday' seems to last for ever, and you are quite ready to get back to work. As an addition, if you did not feel that you would be sufficiently bored, you could 'rent' some really boring people to go with you! The value here is 'time perception'. There is a big difference between 'time' and 'time perception' – that is exactly why a 'watched pot never boils'.

———•———•———

With the development of the quartz movement, all watches tell the time equally well. A $10 child's watch tells time as well as a $10,000 watch. So the value shifts to something else. A watch is one of the few ways in which a man can wear jewellery. A watch now becomes fun (the Swatch) or an opportunity to project an image. I wear a $30 Russian watch (Sekonda) because the face is easy to read – that is the most significant value for me.

———•———•———

Designer water caught on in a big way because diners did not want to drink alcohol (especially at lunch) but did not want to drink soft drinks either (since there were no 'adult' soft drinks). Diners did not want to order tap water because this seemed cheap and unsophisticated. So diners were crying out for 'an expensive way to buy water'. That was provided by bottled water. The more exotic, the higher the value. I have drunk bottled Swedish water in New Zealand. This is almost as far distant as possible – and in a country that has every bit as much pure mountain water as Sweden.

———•———•———

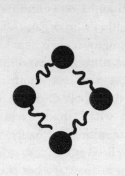

Information is not Enough

Information can provide the routine ways of doing something, or the ingredients for designing value. On the right the information is stacked. On the left is a 'designed' use of information.

Some years ago I wrote a book called *Surpetition*. This was meant to contrast with traditional 'competition'. Competition comes from the Latin and means 'seeking together'. So organizations spend most of their strategic energy looking over their shoulders at the competition. If the competition are cutting prices so should they, etc., etc. I suggested that 'value creation' was more important, and even the creation of 'value monopolies'. Six years after I wrote this book research showed what I had predicted: those organizations that focused on competition did badly, those that focused on value creation did well. Cutting costs, downsizing and efficient housekeeping are often necessary but they are not sufficient long-term strategies. Value creation is essential.

●━━━━●

Information is becoming a commodity. State-of-the-art technology is becoming a commodity. Management competence is becoming a commodity. Price differentials favour less-developed countries. The way forward lies with value creation. This is not a destiny to be 'achieved' but a constant activity.

●━━━━●

In a motor car technological value lasts about six months. After that the technical innovation becomes an 'expectation'. An expectation is very different from a value. You expect power steering to be there and you consider it a defect if it is not there. Such values are not technological improvements but affect other aspects of car use. They include new ways of buying a car (via the Internet); new ways of owning a car (leasing or joint ownership); new ways of parking a car; new ways of insuring a car; new ways of selling a car, etc. I once suggested to Ford (UK) that they should buy a major car-park operator and then restrict parking to Ford cars. 'Integrated values' are values that reside not in the object itself but in the relationship between the object and the user. How does the object 'integrate' into a particular lifestyle? Competition is so old-fashioned that it will continue to be taught at business schools for the next twenty years.

You can send 'repeat orders' to a mail-order house and continue to wear the same clothes as before, which may be elegant, well-cut and suit your personality. But repeat orders do not give you the possibility of change. The identification of standard situations and standard responses by the analysis and judgement habits of the last millennium do not equip us with the design thinking needed for change.

11

The ability to send hundreds of e-mails does not ensure the ability to write something intelligent or amusing.

There are genuine disputes and there are false disputes. It is not at all easy to distinguish between the two, as our traditional thinking habits are the same in each case. A 'false dispute' is a situation where one party is trying it on: 'seeing what you can get away with'; 'using power and bullying to get some advantage'. These are not really disputes at all but forms of aggression. Unfortunately the legal system is not set up to deal with this 'legal aggression'. In the USA, where lawyers derive a fee from what their client wins, there is no risk in 'trying it on'. If you win there is a gain – if you lose there is no loss. Perhaps there needs to be some preliminary court. A deposit could be paid in order to bring a case. If the case is seen to have no merit the deposit would be lost. What about people without much money who could not pay the deposit and for whom the lawyer's contingency fee is so important? In such cases there would be no deposit. Genuine disputes arise from misunderstandings; misinterpretations of agreements; new circumstances; family feuds; genuine conflicts of interest. In family courts around the world there has been a growing trend away from apportioning blame in a strictly legal sense, towards constructing or designing a way forward. The emphasis is less on 'rights' and obligations and more on needs and contribution. The same 'constructive design' approach applies to other situations but is less often used.

●━━━━━●

In any dispute situation there are needs, fears and greeds. All tend to be exaggerated in order to strengthen the point. All tend to be exaggerated because bargaining moves in from the extremes towards the centre. The power of inflicting pain or inconvenience is used as a bargaining force. It is not unlike two male animals posturing in order to achieve dominance. There are threats and counter-threats. Each side claims that the law is on its side, just as in olden days each army claimed that God was on its side. The idiom is strictly adversarial: someone is going to win and the other party is going to lose. The trend today is away from this win/lose idiom to a more win/win outcome. In false disputes this does not work because a party which really deserves nothing is encouraged to try it on in the hope of getting something. That is why it becomes so important to separate out those false disputes and to discourage them. For the win/win approach there is already an excellent system, which is on the statute books in many states in the USA. The parties never meet. There is no bargaining or negotiation. Each side makes its position clear: needs and fears and perceptions. Each side then sets out to 'design' an outcome which would be beneficial or fair to both sides. You are no longer defending your position but 'designing' a way forward. Both designed positions are then put before a judge or a panel. The most 'reasonable' design is then chosen and accepted by both parties. If both parties are indeed making a serious effort to take the other party's needs into account then both outcomes will be 'fair' and it hardly matters which is chosen. You could as well toss a coin. If one party makes no effort to design towards the other party's needs then that design is unlikely to be chosen. If neither party makes a design effort, then both parties are told to go away and to try harder. The concept is excellent – but apparently little used. This is because lawyers are trained in adversarial skills and not in design skills. Each party is also encouraged to believe that a skilled lawyer will get them more than they really deserve – and design will not. It may also be that each party genuinely believes that 'right' is on their side and therefore they should 'win'. Once again this arises from the non-constructive judgement idiom: someone is right and someone must be wrong.

Evolution is not really a 'design' process though it does improve on existing designs. Evolution means that a design produced apparently by random mutation (not very credible) will eventually triumph over an existing design because the new design is better adapted for survival. There is no effort to combine designs to achieve the best of both as there might be in a real design process. Evolution is still a 'triumphant' process, in which one design triumphs over others.

A cyclist towing behind him a rather heavy-looking trailer just kept going and going. He astonished motorists by overtaking them on hills. He never seemed to get tired. The explanation was surprisingly simple. The large trailer contained an electric motor and batteries. The trailer was 'pushing' the cyclist, who just went through the motions of cycling. One of the few things we can do with perception is to try alternative perceptions.

General Motors were very proud of their electric car. You charged up the batteries, drove for about one hundred miles and then charged up the batteries overnight. What a very strange concept. Why not have the electric car towing a trailer full of batteries. When the batteries were discharged you simply change the trailer, as stagecoaches used to change horses. The whole car does not have to sit still while the batteries are being charged. This way the car could go twelve hundred miles in a day, not one hundred miles. Traditional concepts sometimes need challenging.

You are trying to design a better way of paying wages. How can information help? You can look at other schemes in use, both now and in the past. You can compare wages to living expenses. You

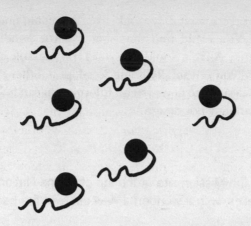

Backwards

The toles are advancing into the future with their gaze fixed on the past. Universities are obsessed with the past and so are most thinkers. The past can provide lessons – but also traps.

could ask workers what they would like. You could find out about grievances. You could find out what experts, pundits and the unions wanted. All this would give you a considerable information base. Unless you are simply going to adopt another system, you still have to design the new system. Information can help in design but information is not design.

(Written at the Mission site at the top of Morne National Park in the Seychelles, with a wonderful view out over the bay)

We may seek a new idea using a 'random word'. This is an incredibly simple technique which seems absurd and illogical but is actually perfectly logical in a patterning universe like the human brain. For example, the word obtained randomly is 'gun'. Guns discharge suddenly but may take longer to load. The suggestion is that a worker could agree to put a portion of his or her wage into a savings account paying higher than normal interest, and could call on this for emergencies or capital payments. Once this idea has been formulated it becomes not unlike the Singapore Central Providence Fund, where employer and worker are required to pay part of the wage into a fund for retirement. This fund can be borrowed against. The idea suggested here is both optional and more flexible. Another concept from the random word 'gun' is that guns have to be aimed at something. The suggestion is that any aimed expenditure (school fees, mortgage, health plans) would be supplemented by the employer. Unallocated expenditure would not. Another concept from 'gun' is that guns usually make a loud noise. This can be heard by all. In some way, general spending habits across the organization might be made known so that the benefits of bulk purchase (insurance, cars, food) could be organized and passed on to the workers. The purpose of this exercise done in a real time of two minutes is not to claim that these are wonderful ideas but to show that creativity and design are not the same as information gathering. Information has a very important part to play in all thinking but no amount of information can take the place of new concepts and design thinking.

———————

Which is the higher value: to have an instant choice of fifty bad movies on your super cable system or to have a choice of only three good movies? Technology enables and that is a value but it is an incomplete value. A state-of-the-art stove in the kitchen and the latest ceramic cooking vessels do not provide a good meal. Could technology deliver a good meal? Possibly; when you put a frozen gourmet dinner in your microwave you might do better than with your own cooking. Improving your own cooking, however, would be even better, with more flexibility and room for invention. The ability to send hundreds of e-mails does not ensure the ability to write something intelligent or amusing. None of this is the fault of technology, which does a wonderful job. It is the fault of those who believe that the momentum of technology will be sufficient. Having a fast car is not the same as having somewhere you want to go.

———————

As a cook, do you deliver traditional dishes with great exactitude or do you experiment and design new dishes? Do cookery schools train you to cook the traditional dishes or teach you how to experiment and how to design new dishes? There is a need for both. As a diner you may not wish to be the first to try a new dish, but as a cook there is joy in a new design that works. All traditional dishes had to be designed at one time unless they gradually evolved one tiny step at a time.

———————

Who invents jokes? This is one of the world's great mysteries. There are places where jokes flourish, such as stock exchanges, the Internet, etc., but where do the jokes originate? To be sure there are skilled gag writers who write for television, radio and film. Maybe these are the only source. Maybe a joke starts out in a mild way and then gets better and better with each telling. I have invented one or two mild jokes and have had them come back to me later. I once set a joke-inventing project on my web site and had some tolerable inventions. A joke is a good example of the design process. Telling old jokes is good fun but hearing a new one is even better.

●————————●

There are those who prefer the old: in furniture, in architecture, in art and in music. It is true that old stuff that has survived must be very good, otherwise it would not have survived. With new stuff there can be mistakes and poor quality because the 'market' has not imposed its discipline. With new stuff it may take time to get used to a new idiom. The Impressionists, who command such a high price today in auction rooms, were at first laughed at and scorned. So there is safety in preferring the old. But how is everything new ever going to emerge if we only worship the old? If we refuse to try any new dish how can cooks be adventurous? There is safety with parents and ancestors but there is excitement with new friends.

●————————●

Museums are both sad places and wonderful places. They are full of the fascination and wonder of the past. Do we have equivalent places devoted to the wonders and possibilities of the future? It was Marshall McLuhan who said that we drive into the future with our eyes on the rear-view mirror. (We met at one o'clock in the morning in Toronto. I was fast asleep when the phone rang. It was Marshall McLuhan, saying that we ought to meet. After comparing our schedules it seemed that the only possible time was right then. So I dressed and took a taxi. We talked until early morning.)

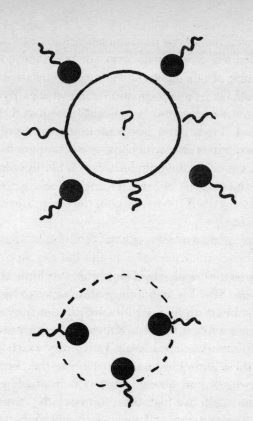

Hypothesis

We do not know what is hidden under the top disc. We can only guess with the hypothesis shown in the bottom circle. Without hypotheses and possibility thinking there can be no progress.

The huge bulk of our intellectual resources are devoted to the past. This is almost the sole occupation of universities. By definition, 'scholars' need something to be scholarly about and that means the past. Book review pages in the more worthy newspapers are at least three quarters filled with books about the past: biographies, period pieces, political memoirs, etc. This is hardly surprising. To write about the past you only need some skill as a writer: the past is there to be described. To write about the future also needs some skill as a thinker.

Some countries are crippled by their history. My homeland, Malta, is one of them. There is such a huge abundance of history going back to the stone age and coming forward through the Phoenicians, Greeks, Romans, Arabs, Spanish, Knights of Malta, French (rather briefly), British and independence. Every step you take you risk bumping into a historic monument. During the Second World War, when digging an air-raid shelter in the back garden, we broke into the tomb of a high-born Roman lady – untouched for almost two thousand years. All this is wonderful, and worth visiting. The downside is that the thinking of the government is that of a museum caretaker – totally unable to look into the future. The past is wonderful and should be preserved, but the past should not be a crippling mental disease.

The trouble with Africa was that it was civilized much too soon. An equilibrium state of tribal civilization was reached. This was based more on interpersonal relations than on technology. There was no need for irrigation so mathematics did not develop. There was no need to travel anywhere so navigation did not develop. There were no lean seasons so storage and astronomy were not needed. The abundance meant that life was very good. Stability

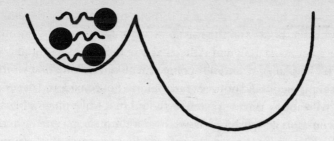

Local Equilibrium

The toles are swimming in a small pond. They need to get out of this to find the much larger pond. We have to disrupt a local equilibrium to reach a more global equilibrium.

was its own reward. Other civilizations triumphed by developing gunpowder, boats and the missionary spirit, followed by commercial exploitation. Ancient Athens also reached a stable state, with much complacency and self-congratulation. It is true that women, slaves and metics did not vote but that was not considered necessary for civilization. Wives were not invited to dinner parties because the commercial geisha girls were more amusing. The Athenian civilization did not produce one single invention. It all came to an end. Complacency without one eye on change and the future is a risky strategy. Yet we all seek such stable tranquillity.

In the Sami (Lapland) culture square buttons on your belt mean you are married; round buttons mean you are single. Recognizing meaning and situations is what judgement is all about. Without judgement we would spend time, effort and energy figuring things out each time. You might be chatting up a comely Lap maiden only to find her jealous husband was eyeing you with suspicion. What about designing a new symbol to indicate that your social interactions were in no sense predatory? The purpose of design is to move forward. The judgement habits of the past millennium keep us out of trouble. The design habits of the next millennium will open up new opportunities.

12

Languages tend to be poor in complex 'perception words' because they are so rich in description possibilities.

There is a wooden ball on a table. You want this ball to get to a certain point. You push with your index finger. It is not at all easy to get the ball to go to where you want it to. Now put the ball on half an inch of foam rubber. You press down with your thumb just ahead of the ball. The ball rolls forward into this depression. The ball will now follow wherever you drag your thumb. Exhortation and pressure are not much use in getting people to do what you want them to do. If, however, the very next step is easy, attractive and available, then that next step will be taken. That next step needs to be 'designed'. We are not good at designing next steps.

●————●

A group of business executives have decided that they want to get to a certain town. Once that decision has been made and agreed upon, getting there is not so difficult. There are cars, road maps, street signs, etc. The decision about the destination is the difficult part. Once the decision has been made implementing it is not difficult. The same group of executives are looking up at a mountain top. They are all agreed that they want to get to the top of the mountain. That is obviously a good place to be. This time, talking about the destination and deciding upon it is no longer enough. You need to learn some climbing skills in order to get to the top of the mountain. This is exactly the case with 'creativity'. All sorts of captains of industry, and other leaders, talk about the huge importance of creativity in the future. Most corporations claim to be 'creative'. Talking about it does not have much effect. You need to do something about it. To climb the mountain you need to learn some climbing skills. Similarly, talking about creativity is not enough, there is a need to learn the skills of creative thinking. There is a need to learn the 'design' idiom of thinking. That is so different from our normal analysis/judgement mode of thinking that some effort is required. Just being 'intelligent' and broadly capable is no longer enough. A superb runner does not automatically become a great swimmer. There is still the need to learn how to swim. An intelligent analytical thinker does not automatically become a creative designer. The idioms are very different. They are not mutually exclusive. You can play good bridge and you can learn to play good poker. They are different games. At any one moment you choose which game to play. Both games are valid. But they are different.

•————•

In one of my books I introduced the concept of the 'logic bubble'. When someone does something of which we do not approve we are quick to condemn that person as stupid, disruptive, difficult, etc. The 'logic bubble' takes the opposite view. The new view is that everyone at all times behaves with impeccable logic. They behave with this logic within their personal 'bubble' of perception, experience, needs and emotions of the moment. So instead of trying to persuade, or force, someone to act differently, you seek to understand their particular logic bubble. Then you make an effort to change perceptions, to change that logic bubble. Skilled sales people probably do this all the time – after all you cannot 'force' someone to buy something. You seek to make it 'intelligent behaviour' for the person to make the purchase. This change in logic bubbles requires some design skill and design energy. Judgement as such is not going to achieve anything. Nannies with young children are very good at changing logic bubbles when they want to get their charges to do something.

•————•

Hybrids, zebras and stews are mixtures. We can recognize that some things are not pure. But we do not like it. There are friends and there are enemies. There are indeed people who are both friend and enemy. Such people may be friendly (and truly friendly) when it suits them and an enemy when that suits them. We can say that such people are 'false friends' or 'fairweather friends' but that is inaccurate – they may always be true friends because it always suits them. The reason 'judgement' does not like stews is that we do not know how to react. We welcome a friend and we steer clear of an enemy. So what do we do about a friend/enemy? It is usually the simplicity of action that forces simplicity on perception. We can perceive complex situations but our range of actions is much more limited. It used to be said that in the British army you only needed to learn two things: if it moved salute it; if it did not move paint it white.

In the Seychelles there seems to be a very efficient bus service. There are dozens of Tata buses running frequently in every direction. These buses are probably very skilfully driven but the appearance of a Tata bus coming around a corner at high speed can terrify a tourist driver. So the word 'tata' could be applied to the complex perception of a large vehicle apparently driving at high speed with scant regard for other motorists. This description is probably very unfair on the driver and also on the excellent Tata buses. It is used as an example of a word created to describe a complex situation. Languages tend to be poor in complex 'perception words' because they are so rich in description possibilities. Description is, however, very different from perception.

In a book I wrote on conflict resolution I suggested the new word 'confliction'. I believe there is a need for such a word. We usually see conflicts when they become apparent as such. Conflicts can, of course, get worse but there is a point at which we can recognize

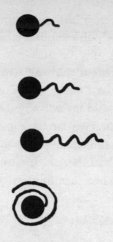

More is Better

The tail of the tole gets longer and longer. Up to a point this might be a benefit. But the end result may be confusion with no useful outcome.

a conflict as such. But before that point there is often, not always, a building-up process which eventually blossoms into a conflict. The parties themselves may or may not be aware of this prior process. It is to this process that the word 'confliction' applies. This is much neater than having to say, each time: 'the process that, if continued, will build up into a real conflict'. If we have the new word 'confliction' then we can have the even more useful word de-confliction' which means taking steps to reduce the confliction. Everyone recognizes that there are situations which build up towards a conflict. Why not capture those situations with a simple perceptual word?

●━━━━●

We are quite good at new words for new things. We have words for computers, Internet, mobile phones, credit cards, microwaves, etc. We are not so good at creating new words for existing situations looked at in a new way. We are not good at creating new words for complex situations. The term 'lateral thinking', which I invented many years ago is now very much part of the language and appears in daily use and in television sitcoms (another new word). It is amazing that it took so very long to develop a word for the sort of thinking that finds a new approach: the sort of thinking that changes concepts and perceptions instead of trying harder with the old ones. Once the word exists we can recognize such situations; we can try to use lateral thinking; we can recognize where it is badly needed; and we can develop formal processes to make it happen on demand.

●━━━━●

The Xhosa language in Africa has eleven different words for the horns of animals: straight up, spiralling, forward bending, backward bending, splaying sideways, etc. Without such a reper-toire of words we would have to use adjectives or phrases which are much weaker perceptually. A painter with a tube of aquamarine colour is more likely to use that colour than a painter who has to

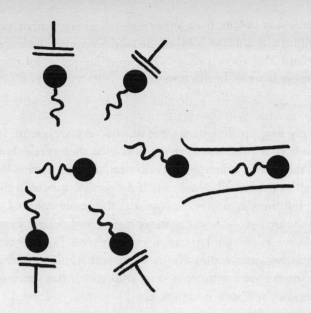

Negativity

In education we use negativity to block paths which do not lead in the 'right direction'. This is like having sheepdogs snapping at the sheep to herd them into the pen.

make up that colour from other colours every time. Complex perception words allow us to see the world in ways which are both richer and also more precise. The new language I have been developing is a step in this direction.

●━━━━━●

Radically new car designs are not always very successful. Buyers may indeed like the new design – and then they think about the resale value. Will other people also like the radical new design? An architect-designed house may have special appeal to the first buyer, but there is always the fear that the resale value of such a special house may be lower than for a standard design. Furniture manufacturers also tend to be conservative – not because of resale values but because people have grown up with traditional furniture. There are no fears with traditional stuff which has been around for ever, but new stuff is high risk.

●━━━━━●

It is said that Sam Goldwyn once chaired a meeting called to discuss new television programmes. At the end of the meeting, with his usual accuracy, he said: 'So we are all agreed – what we need are some brand-new clichés.' Something new – so long as it is the same as the tried and tested. Publishers and movie-makers in the USA are always seeking 'Son of Lassie' and 'Grandson of Lassie' products. The series with Lassie the dog was a great success – so repeat it. It is hard to knock the commercial sense of that attitude, but it does result in rather sterile and boring products. Publishers are as bad with their 'fixed categories'.

●━━━━━●

What is the balance between peace and excitement? What is the balance between security and adventure? What is the balance between sameness and change? What is the balance between the tried and the experimental? What is the balance between yesterday and tomorrow? It has been said that a person with his feet in the oven and his head in the refrigerator is 'on balance' comfortable. It is not a matter of taking an 'in-between' balance position. You cannot play bridge and poker at the same time. You can play both well once you have decided which game you are playing. Nor is it a matter of one group favouring change and another group favouring history. That is the traditional wasteful adversarial position. All players need to know how to play both games and need to have the motivation to play both games. For obvious reasons, the 'history' group (judgement and analysis) have tended to be dominant in our intellectual culture – and they defend that position fiercely with outraged splutterings and sneers. It is time to give more time to the 'design' idiom. You can analyse the past but you need to design the future. Otherwise it may be no better than the past.

In the early days of democracy people used to buy votes. Obviously this was a terrible system. Rich people could buy votes to keep themselves in power so that they could pass laws making them even richer at the expense of those whose votes they had bought. People short of money would sell their political rights just to get food to eat. The wrong sort of people often got elected, because the possession of money did not ensure administrative skills or concepts of social justice. To a lesser extent the system is still in use. Parties with enough money to buy more television time may indeed 'buy' more votes. In a more indirect way, in some countries, people are rewarded after the election for their support. True democracy would suggest true free choice. If a person made the choice to prefer money to political involvement, is that not a true choice (provided hardship and desperation were not involved)? Then we point out that this might be a stupid, short-sighted choice which people might regret later. Is this any different from the usual political choice that is made? There is plenty of room for design improvement in the concept of democracy but change is unlikely because any comment on democracy is seen as a plea for tyranny. And those in power see no purpose in altering a system that has brought them to power. Democracy is not the only sacred cow that cannot be challenged.

●━━━━━━●

Suppose a body of 'wise people' sat in a room and interviewed all parliamentary candidates. These would be given one, two, three or more stars (like hotels). They would be assessed on sincerity, honesty, compassion, ability, economic sophistication, etc. No one would be forced to go to the interviews. Those with low star ratings could choose never to mention this. Those with high ratings might make full use of this endorsement. Would that work? Would that be fair? Voters could choose to ignore the ratings just as they might ignore a newspaper columnist's opinion of a candidate. There is nothing compulsory about it. Those with true ability might welcome this chance to have their ability independently endorsed. I suspect this idea would be mostly rejected because the very messiness of politics with its mix of able and less able, thoughtful and passionate, small-minded and open-minded is what it is all about. There is such a terror of 'direction' that messiness becomes a virtue. People are messy – let them choose a messy government. The value of 'effective government' is not the highest value when considering democracy.

●━━━━━━●

Theoretically it is possible to insert an electrode near the 'pleasure centre' in the brain and to sit in a corner never doing anything more than stimulating this centre. Food and other physical needs would have to be looked after. Assuming that economics could be designed to support such behaviour, would it be acceptable? In some ways it would be no different from drug addiction and alcoholism, except that there might be more choice from moment to moment. As the technology of entertainment and distraction gets ever more powerful we may be moving that way – not with an inserted electrode but with delivered entertainment. Children

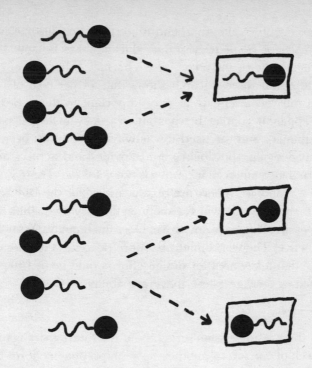

Lumping and Splitting

In the top part toles moving east are lumped together with toles moving west. The underlying similarities are what matters. In the bottom part toles are 'split' into those moving east and those moving west. This distinction is seen as being important.

in some countries already spend more time watching television than at school. Some television is educational to be sure. If that is a person's choice and no one else is harmed, what is wrong with it? At the same time research shows that 74 per cent of young people rate 'achievement' as very important to them. So there is an apparent conflict between increasingly available passive entertainment and the need for activity. Society has been very poor in designing possibilities for activities and achievement – because the commercial incentive is not yet there. There is sport. There are hobbies. There are organizations like the Boy Scouts. Then there are gangs, which sometimes find negative achievement rather easier. Plants are not active. Does the human species 'have' to be active. The world might be more peaceful if it were not. I suspect that a key area for design effort would be 'achievement possibilities' for youngsters of average ability.

●———————●

When there is a television series about the future there is usually high tech of one sort or another: spaceships, phasers, force fields, beam-me-up stuff, etc. Suppose the future were to contain more 'conceptual' matters: perhaps a community that lived in a fulfilled way through new concepts of behaviour and human interaction. That is not likely to happen through evolution or technical inventiveness (though this would help on the supply side). It is more likely to happen through design. I would like to see a series about creatures from another planet who were remarkably stupid – but had one key piece of mental software which pushed them far ahead of humankind.

We can seek to do better and better at what we are doing now – or we can change the way we do something. As a student, Fosbury did not seek to get better and better at the traditional Western-roll method of high jump. Instead he invented the Fosbury flop, which is a different approach. He won the Olympic high jump and changed the method for ever.

13

'What-is' thinking is
concerned with truth.
'What-can-be' thinking is
concerned with value.

The education system in every country is a disgrace. Where are the schools that teach constructive thinking – the most important of all human skills? Where are the schools that teach 'operacy' or the skills of doing? Where are the schools that teach how value is really created in society, by business, by government, etc.? Education is driven by 'continuity' and not by any regard for the needs of individuals or the needs of society.

If you want to see current thinking at its worst pick up almost any newspaper. Somewhere in it will be a piece that mixes advocacy with dishonesty: taking things out of context; selecting information to make a point; and explicit dishonesty. Not every newspaper and by no means every piece of writing, but even the most worthy of newspapers do this from time to time. Pick out 'the shading' words like 'so-called' or 'claims' which are pure expressions of subjective emotions and nothing to do with exploration of the subject. Such pieces treat the intelligence of the readers with contempt – particularly readers who are well-informed on the subject.

If you are taking a dog for a walk and you come to a fork in the road, you have to decide which road to take: the right-hand road or the left-hand road? It is obvious that you cannot walk along both roads at the same time. If you are an investment manager you do not have to decide between investing in bonds or shares.

You can do both at once. Sometimes we set up 'either/or' choices when these are not required. In fact we do not have too much choice because the brain is wired up to give either/or recognition – as in those pictures which flip from one interpretation to another but never show both at once. We find it extremely difficult to hold several 'maybe' positions in mind at the same time. No doubt biological survival needed strong judgements and decisions, which could then be followed by definite action. A fast but wrong decision might be better than a delayed right decision.

• ———— •

Telephone numbers provide a fine example of discrimination. You can pick up a telephone in London and choose a number and talk to one person in the USA out of the many millions who live there. This is a superb example of 'what-is' thinking. To meet new people, however, you might have to try the Internet, which opens up possibilities.

• ———— •

The brain seeks to adapt to and to learn about the world as it is. How could it adapt to future 'possible worlds'? The better we are at adapting, the less motivated might we be to design changes. To design changes you need to have a strong sense of 'value'. You need to have a strong sense of the value that is not there, or insufficiently there.

• ———— •

'What-is' thinking is concerned with truth; 'what-can-be' thinking is concerned with value. There is value in truth. There is value in finding out how the villagers make bean soup and repeating that recipe. There is also truth in value. If you decide to put Pernod in pumpkin soup you get a fine new taste – that is truly a fine taste. It all depends on which we aim for first.

In assessing the importance of inventions, do you look at the mass impact or the direct significance? If you need a cardiac pacemaker, then that is the most important invention possible. The father of nuclear energy (Enrico Fermi) opened up an amazing source of ultimate energy. But what impact does that have on most people's lives? In France 80 per cent of electricity comes from nuclear plants but this is not so elsewhere. It is possible that the horror of nuclear war has made major wars impossible in the future – so most people benefit. The inventor of the bra (Mary Phelps Jacob) has made life more comfortable for millions of women. The inventor of frozen foods (Clarence Birdseye) has also affected the lives of millions. The inventor (Marcian Hoff) of the microchip opened up computing and put computing power in many devices. What about the inventor of the rapidly growing Internet (Tim Berners Lee)? Yet the inventor of a catheter to remove clots from blood vessels is said to have saved fifteen million lives. How many lives has the Internet saved? Inventions are designs. Inventions are the putting together of principles and materials to deliver a value. The value may be a life-or-death value for a few people, or it may be increased comfort or convenience for a large number of people.

●━━━●

What is particularly interesting about inventors is that they rarely make just one invention. Many have hundreds of patents to their name. Edison had 1,093 patents. Joseph Gerber had 650 patents. Both Edwin Land and Jerome Lemelson had 500 patents.

●━━━●

Mrs Lillian Gilbreth, a pioneer in ergonomics, was a mother of twelve who made a large number of inventions. Is it that the motivation to invent was always urging them to challenge existing methods and to design better ones? Is it that the confidence,

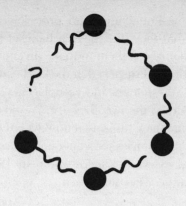

Completion

There is an urge to complete our thinking about something. This is
called 'closure'. We want the comfort of tying things together.

and success, of the initial invention propelled them to further inventions? Is it that they developed a habit of mind and a way of thinking which enabled them to make inventions? All of these factors may contribute. I suspect that the key factor is the 'opposite of complacency'. We understand complacency, which is a lazy satisfaction with things the way they are. We do not have a word which describes an innate 'dissatisfaction' with the way things are. Why should it take centuries for someone to invent the bra? The bra was invented by Mary Phelps Jacob in 1913 because she wanted to wear a sheer evening gown.

●━━━━━●

It has always been said that 'necessity is the mother of invention'. Chester Carlson invented the Xerox copy process because he was arthritic and near-sighted and his job was to make, by hand, duplicate copies of patent applications. There was a need to make copies in a better way. At other times the invention has come long before the need. The laser (Gordon Gould) was a marvellous invention with no immediate use. Later the uses multiplied and every CD player (invented by James Russell) now depends on a laser reader. Scientific thought may move forward and create a design. It may then be a matter of looking around for a 'value application' for that design. The momentum of science and technology pushes forward. It is up to inventors to design value from the new possibilities. Prior need is by no means the only source of value. Did anyone really conceive of a need for X-rays before they were developed?

●━━━━━●

Design does not have to be as specific or as original as an invention. Cooking a meal is a design process if it is not routine. Presenting the meal is a design process. Anything that is not repeated routine is a 'design'.

Almost everyone would like to change the QWERTY layout of letters on a keyboard. This was designed to slow down typing when fast typing made the letters jam. But now we are locked into that system and everyone trains to use it, so change is resisted. We can be locked in by adequacy.

14

In any self-organizing information system we know that there is a mathematical necessity for provocation.

Problem-solving may involve design. The usual approach to problem-solving is to identify and remove the cause of the problem. Sometimes this is not possible because the cause cannot be found; because there are too many causes; or because the cause is human nature and cannot be removed. In such cases we are usually paralysed. Most of the major problems in the world will not be solved by more analysis. There is a need for design. There is a need to design a way forward – leaving the cause in place. Design, however, is very much more than problem-solving. A design may deliver a new value that has not been thought of before. A design may be a better way of delivering an existing value. Design is a matter of putting things together to deliver a value. What 'truth' is to analysis, 'value' is to design.

●━━━━━●

We have used pencils for years. How much thought has been given to the design of the 'grip' on a pencil? Perhaps a better grip is not possible because people hold pencils in many different ways. Perhaps any attempt to provide a grip would raise the production cost too much. Perhaps everyone is quite happy with the way things are. There are a lot of reasons why things do not improve. The main reason is that there does not seem to be any need for improvement.

●━━━━━●

It is not difficult to see why we put such a high value on negativity. In school the teacher has to point out 'why something is wrong'.

To do anything else would risk misleading the students, who do need to know some things. The teacher often asks a pupil to point out why something suggested by another pupil is wrong. The asked pupil does so with great glee. The greatest joy of intellectuals in the Athenian civilization was to compose clever, malicious speeches attacking one another. School debate is encouraged. Perhaps 'attacking' verbally is no different from other sorts of attack and pleasing in a jungle sort of way. It hardly needs saying that being negative gives a very easy sense of superiority and requires none of the much more difficult constructive effort. Which is easier: to make a beautiful Murano wineglass – or to smash it?

●━━━━━━━●

If animals were not born with an inbuilt instinct to do things 'the right way' they would never survive. Could a spider work out how to build an intricate web from scratch or through the instruction of an older spider? Could a colony of termites figure out how to build a termite mound with its indoor gardens? So doing things 'the right way' is rather important. Where would the impulse to do things in a 'better way' come from? There is no such impulse in the animal world – and not much of it in the human world. How do you know something is right unless it is not new – and can therefore be compared with the old?

●━━━━━━━●

How does a finger know how to grow? How does a growing leaf know what to do next? It does not. The combined chemical effects around it (the chemical field and gradients) make the next step inevitable. There is no choice. There is no alternative – unless something goes wrong. So it is with most of our behaviour. The surrounding circumstances choose the established patterns and we proceed down that path. The less thinking the better, because at best thinking is uncertain and at worst unpleasant. Least-effort survival is more important than risky innovation. So judgement is better than design.

New varieties of roses are being designed all the time. The colours are deeper and the petals fuller and more perfect. On my island in Venice I have a wide variety of such 'designed' roses. The most powerful scent, however, comes from the oldest roses, which were not 'designed'. Too often the search for one set of values means that other values are lost.

Some of the best-tasting tomatoes in the world are to be found on the small island of Malta. There is a real tomato taste about them. They taste very much better than the tomatoes to be found in supermarkets in most countries. Tomatoes have been designed and bred to be large, firm, good in colour, to keep well in storage and to have a good weight. The designs have been successful – but the taste has suffered. Tomatoes must look good in the supermarket and must continue to look good. Taste is a lesser consideration – especially as everyone will soon have forgotten what tomatoes should taste like.

What should well-designed clothes do? Should they advertise the designer – overtly or on inquiry? Should they enhance the self-image and confidence of the wearer? Should they make a desired impression on others? Should they be comfortable? Should they be flexible enough to be worn on many occasions? Should they be striking and noticeable? Should they be elegant and understated? Should they advertise class, wealth or a pretence at these? You choose your value or values and design to deliver them. Usually you need to trade off one value against another.

Very few tax systems are designed as a whole. Bits and pieces get added all the time to satisfy immediate political needs and

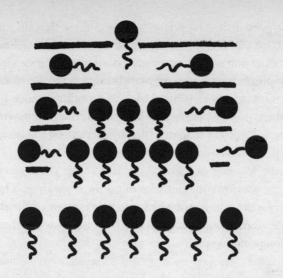

Education Filters

At each stage people are filtered out. Very few make it to the top. The system is designed for the few who make it, not for the many who do not.

economic pressures. The result is often a mess that no one really wants. Loopholes are discovered and used, and then have to be plugged. Plugging a loophole may create an injustice elsewhere. Higgledy-piggledy and incremental changes rarely produce a good design – too often there is no choice. If a political move is seen to disadvantage poorer people, such as an increase in cigarette tax, then there is a need to 'balance' this by increasing the tax on more wealthy people. When the government of Margaret Thatcher reduced the top rate of income tax from over 80 per cent to 40 per cent she was undoing decades of political juggling. The design of the very next step is not always to the benefit of the design of the whole. Expediency may design the next step: effectiveness should design the whole.

•————•

What does it matter what a house looks like, since when you are living in it you rarely see the outside? Maybe the outside will impress your friends and neighbours. Maybe the outside will attract buyers – including yourself. In the end the outside is the 'image' of the house that exists in your mind. So the design is not for cost or convenience but for image.

(On board QF 2307 from Cairns to Mackay)

Who decides what design is acceptable or what design is best? Time is a great decider, either through evolutionary pressures or by letting people get used to a new design. Once upon a time, in Athens, King Paul and Queen Frederika called the architects together to tell them that the royal pair did not like the buildings that were being built. The architects protested: 'Who is to decide on taste,' they asked. Queen Frederika replied, 'We do.' This story was told to me directly by Queen Frederika as we sat side by side on a Qantas flight from Bombay (now Mumbai) to London. She

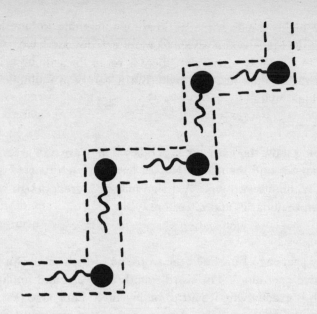

The Next Step

Things get done if the very next step is designed to be obvious and easy. There should be no uncertainty, no doubt and no complexity. The toles change direction at each angle – that is all.

was a highly intelligent lady. There is something to be said for single decisions about style. Committees do not have style – individuals do. It is true that there is room for a multiplicity of styles rather than just one style. But it can be a multiplicity of individual styles.

●━━━━━━●

At a dog show there are great poodles. There are also great Irish wolfhounds and great Jack Russell terriers. Each type of dog is great within its own type. A design may be a great design within its own boundaries and intentions.

●━━━━━━●

Many years ago I invented the word 'po', which stands for 'provocative operation'. The word sounds awkward and unnatural, which is exactly why it had to be invented. Language describes the world the 'way it is'. A provocation is a statement that is outside or contrary to our experience. We might say: 'Po a car has square wheels.' This statement is not only contrary to our experience but goes against the very purpose of wheels. So why is there a value in that provocation? In any self-organizing information system we know that there is a mathematical necessity for provocation. Otherwise matters settle down in a 'local' equilibrium. A provocation destabilizes that equilibrium so that we increase the chance of moving to a more 'global' equilibrium. With square wheels we would get a bumpy ride as the wheels rotated on to their corners. This could be anticipated and the suspension could compensate. From this we get the concept of suspension which reacts 'in anticipation of need'. This then becomes a vehicle for moving over very rough ground. Just as a human would raise his or her legs when running over rough ground so the car would raise the wheels. This is a perfectly practical process which has been tried out. The car remains stable but the wheels follow the profile of the ground. So we move from a provocation to a perfectly sound idea. There is a logic in the apparent illogicality of a provocation. The formal use of provocations is part of lateral thinking. We do not judge a provocation, because that would be nonsense. Instead we use a different mental operation. This is the operation of 'movement'. Judgement is based on 'is' or 'is not' – depending on whether something matches our experience or does not match our experience. Movement is based on 'to': where does this take us to?

●————●

We badly need a new word to cover 'the broad concept', 'the general concept' or 'the approach'. When we set out to do something our minds first think of the very broad concept. This is then narrowed down and ends up with a practical idea. If some water is spilled on the floor we think of 'some way of mopping it up'. We then proceed to think of a mop, a towel or some tissues. When this problem was put to some young children one six-year-old suggested putting sugar in the water and having the dog lick it up. This was a broader concept than 'mopping': it was the concept of 'removing' the water. Perhaps we could invent the word 'framco' to indicate the 'framing concept'. We then work out the details within this frame. If you want to change the frame then you change the framco. The need, however, is not acute, as words like 'approach' do tolerably well, so I do not expect this word to catch on.

●————●

What is your perception? What is your view? How do you see things at this moment? This is an extremely important part of thinking and of design thinking. The way we are looking at something determines all subsequent thinking. That is why most of the errors of thinking are errors of perception. Many years ago I invented the word 'popic' to mean 'the possible picture seen at this moment': 'What is your popic here?'

●————●

Designs could produce many possibilities. How do we select the best possibility to pursue? The simplest selection procedure is an 'emotional' choice: which one do we like? Once the emotional choice has been made, then fuller examination in terms of risk, downside, cost, benefits, etc., can be done. The narrowing down from a large number of possibilities to a few that can be examined more fully, can indeed be emotional (which includes aesthetic). If the decision is to be made by a group rather than an individual, then the emotional approach simply does not work. The selection framework might then consist of four points: benefits, feasibility, cost and testing. The benefits need to be spelled out with as much supporting data as possible; if the value is poor, then the design is poor. Then comes 'the ease of doing'. Can this be done easily? Are there mechanisms or channels in place for doing this? Assuming that there are benefits and the design can be done, then it is a matter of looking at costs. An assessment of costs includes: money, time, hassle, attention, resources, opportunities foregone, etc. The final consideration might be 'ease of trying'. If an idea can easily be tried out, at low cost, then the idea is more attractive.

Any new idea that does not raise a howl of protest is probably not a good idea. Those who are comfortable in the use of the old idea find it difficult to see the inadequacies of the old idea. If you have to imagine new benefits and you cannot achieve this effort of imagination, you have no choice except to resist the new.

15

It is precisely because judgement is so important, and such an excellent activity of both the human brain and human culture, that it is necessary to point out the dangers.

In the news there is a spate of shootings and killings by gunfire. We assume this is by tough, callous, violent macho types. That may be true – but the opposite may also be true. Maybe it is the timid, weak drop-outs who are doing the killing. These are the types who carry weapons to defend themselves, because they cannot rely on brute force. These are the types who cannot cope with life and are driven to desperation. These are the types who have to prove themselves. To join certain gangs and to show you are tough you are required to go out and kill someone. Judgement assumes that it must be the tough types who disregard the law and live by violence. It is difficult for judgement to accept that this may be true but that the opposite (timid types) may also be true at the same time. The reason judgement finds this hard is that if judgement is not 'discriminatory', then it is useless. It is difficult for judgement to say: 'This plant is a deadly poison – at the same time this plant is good for you.' As a matter of fact this is exactly the case with digitalis, which is one of the most powerful and most used drugs for treating heart failure. It is also a deadly poison – if too much is taken.

●━━━━━●

Protagoras was one of the Sophist thinkers who were so despised by Plato and his followers. This was partly because the Sophists were provincial, and the Athenians believed that country bumpkins could not think. In fact, Protagoras was quite a modern system thinker. He pointed out that manure put on the leaves of a plant killed the plant but manure put on the roots made the plant grow

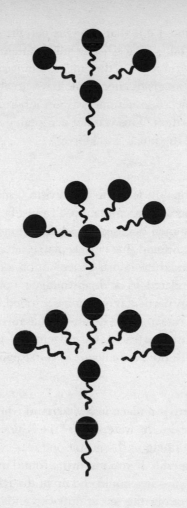

More of the Same

New ideas are often no more than old ideas dressed up. If we know
that the old idea worked, then a 'new', more elaborate version will
also work. This is the progress from the arrangement at the top to
that at the bottom.

strongly. He pointed out that giving a certain substance might cure the patient but giving twice as much might kill the patient. Similarly the same amount of the same substance given now might cure the patient but given later would have no effect. He pointed out that the 'value' of something was not inherent but depended on the whole situation. This was not acceptable to the Platonists, who emphasized the inner 'ideal form'.

●————————————●

System-based thinking leads to 'relativism', and this has been firmly rejected because it can be used to justify many things. In some cultures women accused of adultery might be stoned to death by a mob. Should this be acceptable because it is 'part of that culture'? Should the courts be lenient on a criminal because the crimes are related to a disadvantaged upbringing? While self-defence on any particular occasion is justified, should a child be allowed to kill a brutal parent? Relativism has no finite boundaries. This makes it a threat to traditional judgement – which is a 'digital system' (on or off), not an analogue system (quantity).

●————————————●

It is said that there is a place in Switzerland where you stand on a ridge which divides the watershed of the Rhine from that of the Danube. If it is raining and you spit one way, your saliva could end up in the Danube. If you just turn around and spit the other way (no wind) your saliva could end up in the Rhine. The Rhine and the Danube enter the sea at opposite ends of Europe. The nerve networks in the brain operate in a somewhat similar way. Two things which appear quite similar may end up being treated very differently. Two villages a few hundred yards from each other may have very different dialects and even languages. The explanation is that each village developed from an inland spread of riverside settlements on rivers which are actually far apart. The villages are really back to back. Because of its characteristics, the design of the brain makes it excellent for fine discriminations. In my psychology finals at Oxford University I met a builder who could discriminate, visually, angles which were only two degrees different.

•———————•

There seems to be almost an inbuilt motivation to 'discriminate'. Maybe it is just the natural functioning of the brain as it permits us to learn our way around a complex world. Psychologists love to devise tests which put people into different boxes. The tests are refined and have high repeat reliability – but not much practical value. The tests can be so good that even a slight difference in performance puts people into very different categories. In practice that slight difference in performance is not important. Also, if the variance is high, then the overall results of the test may be valid but cannot be applied with much confidence to a particular individual. Boys are supposed to be better at maths than girls: does that mean that this boy is better than this girl at maths?

•———————•

It may seem that I am being too judgemental about judgement. It is precisely because judgement is so important, and such an excellent activity of both the human brain and human culture, that it is necessary to point out the dangers. If it were not so excellent it would not be used much and there would be no need to point out the limitations. Judgement continues to be excellent – just as the front left wheel of a motor car is excellent. But it is not enough.

•———————•

Something is supposed to be at rest unless there is an imbalance of forces acting on that something. If nothing else, there is the force of gravity. There are two parachutists. One of them is hung up in a tree. The other one is falling at a steady speed through the air. The net forces on both parachutists are zero. They are both the same in this respect. So why is one of them moving? The

155

answer is quite straightforward, but it illustrates one of the dangers of judgement: comparing things in only one aspect.

● ━━━━━ ●

Judgement needs things to be permanent, static and unchanging. Judgement is not much good with things that are continually changing. Judgement is not much good with non-linear systems. Judgement is not much good in feedback situations.

● ━━━━━ ●

There is a much-used story about a frog put into a pan of water. The water is very slowly heated. The frog is boiled to death. I doubt whether the story is true, and I am not about to test it. The point of the story is that the change, from moment to moment, is so slow that at no point does the frog 'judge' it hot enough to jump out of the pan. Judgement needs hard edges.

● ━━━━━ ●

The Internet makes buying and trading shares accessible to everyone. There has developed a breed of 'day traders' who sit in front of computer screens and buy and sell shares all day. They never hold any stocks overnight. These people are not so interested in underlying values as in the potential movement of a share – as driven by other people like themselves. This makes stock-market operations even more of a gamble than most people have always supposed. This may not be entirely fair. The day traders are indeed making 'skilled' judgements. It is just that they are judging something different. Instead of judging the performance of a corporation set against the general economic trends, the day traders are judging 'the reactive behaviour of other people similar to themselves'. They are not judging economic reality but the 'perception' of reality. This is no different from many other situations.

● ━━━━━ ●

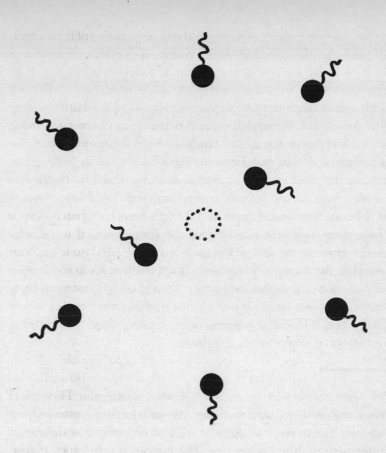

Value Sensitivity

The value is at the centre. The toles on the periphery can sense the value and are headed towards it. The toles in the middle are insensitive to value.

When people go to a restaurant there are many ways in which they choose their food from the menu. A person may choose a dish for which the restaurant is famous. A person may rule out all the dishes he or she cannot eat (pork, spicy, fried, etc.) and be left with a limited choice. A person may choose for health reasons: low cholesterol, like ostrich meat. A person may choose something with which he or she is very familiar. A person may just feel like a particular dish at that moment: like a juicy steak. A person may choose the most exotic dish and something which he or she has never come across before. I once ordered 'mountain oysters' in Mexico and found them to be bull's testicles. The frame of 'judgement' sets the outcome of the judgement. That is why criticism is so easy and so cheap as an intellectual exercise. You just shift the frame of judgement. That dress is stark and boring (if you choose an elaborate frame). That dress is vulgar and fussy (if you choose a simple frame). Since nothing can possibly satisfy all frames, this sort of judgement is absurdly easy. A sprinter is not stayer. A stayer is not a sprinter.

●━━━━━●

We see what we want to see. We see what we are prepared to see. We see what we are used to seeing. We see what our emotions have sensitized us to see. Outside science and objective measurement, judgement is always subjective. The famous psychologist, Piaget, gave children a liquid in a shallow glass and then poured the liquid into a tall thin glass (or vice versa). The children claimed that the liquid in the thin glass was more. Piaget condemned this as failure to understand the concept of 'conservation of volume'. The children were, however, operating the more useful concept (in their own lives) of 'the higher the liquid in the glass, the more the liquid'. This is a very practical concept. But Piaget had his own agenda.

●━━━━━●

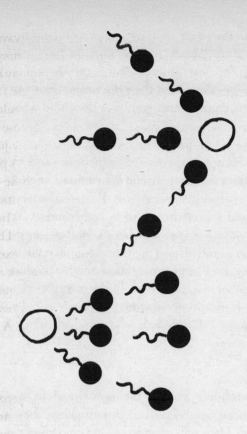

Concepts

Many things come together to form a 'concept', as is shown at the top. A concept can be carried out in many different ways, as is suggested at the bottom. Concepts are important for design.

Wine connoisseurs and art critics have their own frames of reference. They 'know' what to look for and have the verbiage to support complex descriptions. This is mostly skill with a certain amount of hype. Finer and finer discriminations can be made as your experience grows and you have been told what to look for.

●━━━●

In a steady and unchanging world experience and learning would give us ever finer and more useful discriminations. We would learn to find our way around very expertly. We would not create anything new but would survive and have a rather enjoyable life – if the world was not too crowded. There is nothing in the judgement process which would help us put things together. Chance, accident, mistake, play and experimentation might produce something which is then 'seen' to be useful. This is a very weak process. How much more rapid progress would be if we actually learned the process of 'design'. Judgement is 'keeping afloat'; design is 'swimming to the shore'.

●━━━●

If you ask executives, even in the most illustrious of corporations, what areas need new ideas and new thinking, they have not the faintest idea. They will search around and then produce some very broad generalities: to be more productive; to get more customers, etc. Or, they will simply give a list of 'problems'. If you ask the same executives to give you a list of problems, they will do so without hesitation. Problems attract thinking attention. Areas that are not problems do not get any thinking.

●━━━●

There seem to be two sorts of fiction. In the first sort you know exactly what the characters are like. Tarzan will always be Tarzan. Donald Duck will always be Donald Duck. John Wayne was always John Wayne. The interest arose from how they interacted with other characters or with difficult circumstances. Thrillers fall into this category. In the other sort, the reader watches as complex characters unfold and even change. The reader is asked to identify with different situations and feelings. The first sort is 'pantomime' and the second sort is 'psychological drama'. Judgement likes the good guys to be good and to stay good. Complex richness of character can only be judged as 'complex richness of character'. You cannot then predict behaviour – except to say it might be unpredictable.

•————•

In every hotel room in Australia there is equipment for making tea or coffee. This is not the case all around the world. I was in an upmarket hotel in Germany and could not find any way of making tea. To be sure there was room service but this always takes too long. So I looked around for a 'container that would stand heat'. From this concept I went to the specific idea of an emptied can of Coca Cola. Then I needed a 'heat source'. From this concept I went to a candle: cut into thirds and placed together. Then I needed to 'suspend the can over the heat'. A thread tied to the extended handle of my luggage (placed on a table) provided the idea. So I could make my own tea whenever I wanted to. In all the steps the 'general concept' comes first and then a search for a way of carrying out that concept.

•————•

For three thousand years drinking glasses have been more or less the same shape with a circular rim. We can challenge this circularity – not because it is a problem but because we want to challenge it. We came up with the idea of a kite-shaped rim. This is round and wide at one end but comes to a point at the other end (rather like an overhead view of a jug). What are the benefits of this change in shape? If you want to drink a lot of wine, you drink from the wide end. If you want to sip, taste and savour your wine you drink from the narrow end. This is not problem-solving, because there was no problem to solve. It is value creation. There are other things that have been around for three thousand years that could also be improved. That will not happen if we only go around problem-solving.

The Central American cultures never used the wheel because they may have had something better than a wheel. At slow speeds 'bouncing' motion is far more effective than a wheel.

16

Maybe thinking is uncomfortable. Maybe we are biologically programmed to want to 'complete' our thinking as soon as possible.

We have the word 'disagreeable', which is the opposite of agreeable. We have the word 'disgruntled', which is the opposite of the rarely used word 'gruntled'. We have the word 'distressed', which does not seem to be the opposite of 'stressed'. Is 'dismayed' really the opposite of 'mayed'? Words take off on their own because there is a 'situation need' for that word. The term 'lateral thinking' was accepted because there was a situation need for that term. Sometimes we need a word for a situation that does not yet exist because we do not yet look at things that way. But if we could invent the word then we might get to look at things that way. There are a lot of people who are good people but who collapse or turn nasty under stress. It would be unfair to judge them as 'bad'. It would also be risky to judge them as 'good'. We might say 'fragile' or 'unreliable', but those words are too vague. We need a new word which would allow us to look fairly at such people. The difference between judgement and design is that judgement deals with what we have experienced whereas design allows us to create new experiences and new perceptions.

I met this slender feminine woman with a deep, husky, sexy voice. I congratulated her on her voice. Later, someone told me that the person had been a man who had changed sex. Which perception was the more fair: the initial one, or the informed one?

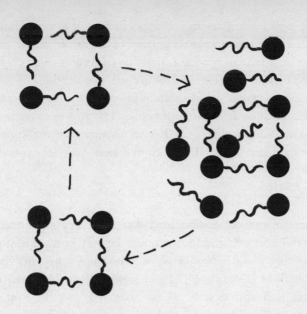

Belief Truth

You see what you are prepared to see. So the 'square' is seen in the jumble of tole activity. Seeing this square reinforces the belief in the square.

The Italians have a saying: 'If it is not true it is well found (*ben trovato*).' This seems an elastic version of 'truth'. In fact it allows a story to be accepted for itself (perhaps making a point), whether it is true or not. In Venezuela there are two versions of time. In the ordinary version you are sometimes very late. But if you specify *ora ingles*, then you are exactly punctual. This two-tier system works well. In the Bahamas there is 'Roosevelt' time and real time. One is later than the other. If you know where you are, you do not fret.

●━━━━●

The central railway station in Tokyo is a very large place. So when your host tells you that you will 'be met' you wonder where that meeting is going to take place. The train stops and you step off. Your host is standing right in front of you. He knew which seat you had and exactly where that 'seat' would stop. Such precision makes life very much easier. The great value of the judgement system is to provide both precision and prediction. There may be nothing new but a wonderful organization of what is not new. A good classification system in a library allows you to find with ease exactly the book you want. It is said that computer medical diagnosis is 99 per cent as good as a real doctor. Perhaps if humankind could be relieved of this sort of thinking we could spend more time on the creative and design side. Computers can do 'optimizing' designs but not (yet) concept-changing designs.

●━━━━●

Stick insects do not 'need' males. The female can produce new females without being fertilized by any male. Are they missing anything? They are missing gene-mixing, which might be a value if the genes are weak. How do we get 'idea mixing' when there is total complacency about rather feeble ideas?

Why do we have shoe sizes? Why not have a cobbler measure your feet and make shoes to fit you exactly? Shoe size is a judgement of your foot size matched with a judgement of a manufacturer's offering. That way you can get a wider offering of styles at a much cheaper price. Money is a judgement of your effort and a judgement of a reward system. Money allows for a much greater flexibility than paying your petrol station in chickens or haircuts. Most judgements have the same function. A university degree is a judgement that this person is able and knows something about the subject (even if not much about thinking). An employer accepts this judgement just as an employer may accept a personal reference – which is also a judgement. A world without judgement would be very hard work, very chaotic, very unfair – and, occasionally, creative. If not the personal cobbler, the shoe-store assistant would have to try dozens of shoes to get a fit.

●————●

In school, if the pupil does not give the standard, expected, answer then that pupil is 'wrong'. Yet the pupil's answer may be better or just different. If, instead of standard answers, we relied on the teacher's personal judgement in each case, then for some teachers the result would be much better, but for others it would be a great deal worse. The idiosyncratic judgements of different teachers might get pupils begging for standard answers. If there were no standardized laws (and sentences) then transgressors would have to depend on the personal preferences and prejudices of individual judges and magistrates. If there were no standard diseases most of us would not be here. Standards mean judgement.

●————●

Should judges make laws by setting a precedent of a creative 'interpretation' or should law-making be left to Parliament. Maybe Parliament does the coarse tuning and judges do the fine tuning.

Any law has to be interpreted and applied. Where the law is codified, judges still make interpretations, but these do not set precedents. How fat is fat? You could set an artificial weight limit but this would be unfair on 'big people'. So you set an average for age, height and sex and then treat as 'fat' significant deviations from this average. That process is much more difficult with behaviour where behaviour (outside of sport) is more difficult to measure.

(Sheraton Mirage, Gold Coast, Queensland, Australia; Lotus conference)

What is the purpose of examinations in schools? The main purpose might be to motivate students to work hard and take their studies seriously. If nothing else, the examinations are a feedback system to both parents and the students themselves. Another purpose might be to test whether or not the student has achieved some competence level in that subject. This last judgement is very complex and includes the following considerations. Was the examination a good test of knowledge in that subject? Some students get a sense of the 'usual questions' and study these – so doing well in the examination without really knowing the subject. Is the examination a test of the student's ability or of the teacher's ability in teaching that subject? Is the examination a test of the student's general ability or of the student's interest in that particular subject? Is the examination a test of the student's general intelligence or the ability to remember the sort of information which examinations demand? We find it easy to set up judgement systems, which can have a serious impact on a person's life, but are not really sure what we are judging.

●━━━━━━●

It is possible to create a psychological test which some people answer in one way and others answer in another way. That test can be refined and the more 'discriminating' questions can be extracted to increase the sensitivity of the test. But what are we testing? Those taking the test have an idea of their 'desired self-image' or the required idiom. So they respond accordingly. To guard against this it is possible to insert 'trick questions'. The ultimate labelling, boxing, discrimination, may seem very concrete even if the basis for it is rather fragile. Where results in a test correlate directly with results in a particular field, then that test may be a useful predictor of current ability in that field. It is important to note the word 'current'. If a field currently does not require creativity, then a person with low creative motivation may do well. But if the field is changed to require more initiative, then the test may no longer be valid. The danger arises when the test is not used as a predictor of performance in a specific field but of a more general quality such as 'intelligence'. The original purpose of IQ tests was to see how young children compared with their peers. If the young children had all been exposed to the same background and influences, then differences were assumed to arise from some innate ability. Where the backgrounds were not the same, then the test might have been testing the background (also useful). It is the blurring of all these considerations (at least in lay eyes) which causes confusion. What does 'intelligence' mean? Does it mean the ability to do well in 'intelligence tests'? Does it mean the ability to do well in real life? Does it mean the ability to do anything well, or just the sort of things to be found in intelligence tests? Such questions are asked over and again. Testing how quickly a car accelerates is valid – but only one part of general performance. There is also road-holding, braking, steering, fuel economy, crash safety, etc. That is why the notion of 'emotional intelligence' came about. Even this is inadequate as a measure of potentially useful behaviour.

●━━━━━━●

We like judgement because judgement is so important and so useful. No judgement is bad. Some judgement is good. More judgement is better. So even more judgement must be better still? This need not be so. We come to the downward part of the salt curve: more and more salt is worse and worse.

●━━━━━━●

The best test of creativity is not a pencil-and-paper test but the real-life use of creativity. A major corporation found that if they asked people to name the creative people amongst their workmates, there was good agreement. If you work alongside people, you know who is always coming up with ideas. You know who to go to if you have a problem. You know who likes to generate and consider alternatives. Though far less practical, this 'in-use' assessment of creativity is far more valuable and a much better predictor of creative performance than a paper-and-pencil test.

●━━━━━━●

Design makes use of 'standard known elements'. An architect knows the strength of that steel or that concrete. An architect knows the water-resistant qualities of a material. An architect does not have to start with zero knowledge. Design is a matter of putting together current knowledge to deliver new value. If it is not 'new value', then a standard routine response would suffice.

●━━━━━━●

Music makes use of standard notes. It is the way the standard notes are put together that creates the value of that piece of music. Design is not the opposite of information, standard responses, judgement, etc. Most people have never mixed marmalade and Marmite (Vegemite in Australia) on a piece of toast, though both are standard products. The taste is attractive because bite is added to the marmalade. There are many cooks who can produce standard dishes with great expertise. There are fewer cooks who can design new dishes. You need to be able to imagine tastes and their combinations. A strategy of 'random mix and try' might produce some new ideas but it would be a very slow process.

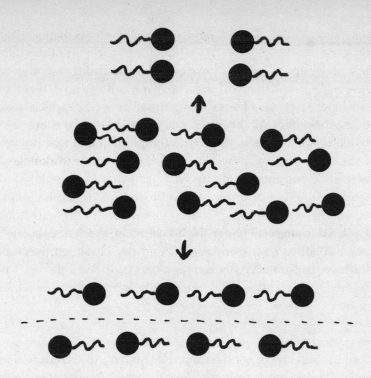

Analysis and Design

The middle part shows toles moving in every direction. Analysis can analyse this movement into an eastward movement and a westward movement. Design goes further and sets up a system so the toles moving in opposite directions do not interfere with each other.

At an early age a child has to be busy with designing responses to the world. Certain standard elements (like bawling) are put together to achieve an effect. This is design through ignorance which leads to improvisation. As the child gets older, he or she learns the standard, adult or 'right way' to do things. In almost all cases this is the most efficient, proven and tried method. So the 'design' motivation and aptitude die away.

If you ask youngsters under the age of ten to draw a spacecraft, they will design their own design. After the age of ten they will draw a rocket with NASA written on the side. We think we like children to be children. Children usually prefer to become adults as soon as possible.

Design is a matter of consideration. If you have to stand naked in front of a shower in order to adjust the water temperature there is surely something very wrong. You get scalded and frozen before you reach the appropriate mix of hot and cold water. If the controls of an airline seat are placed exactly where you rest your elbows then the seat will be constantly going backwards and forwards 'of its own accord'. No matter how good a design might be with regard to other values, if there is a lack of consideration of 'use factors' the design is a poor design.

A lot of effort is put into designing ways of shopping by telephone and over the Internet. Little thought is given to a key part in the design. You can choose, order and pay for the goods – but how are you going to receive them? If both partners are working and there is no one at home, how are the goods to be delivered? There is a need to design a 'collection point' system. All goods would be delivered to that point (perhaps a petrol station) and could then be collected in one car journey.

•——————•

I once suggested the design of a special hat shaped like a biretta or mortarboard, with four sides. There would be a tassle attached at the top in the centre. If you wore the tassle hanging to the left side it might mean: 'I am unattached and looking to meet someone.' If you wore the tassle to the right side it would mean: 'Leave me alone. Don't hassle me. I am in a secure relationship, etc.' The tassle worn in front or worn behind would also have their own specific meanings. This 'visual signalling' would have its value – and also its dangers. To prevent the wind deciding your 'avail- ability' there would have to be some way of fixing the tassle, such as a clip. I believe there is a radio chip, in Japan, which allows people with compatible search profiles to locate each other in a night club. Whether these sorts of things are desired values or not, clearly there is a value created. In both instances the technology is not difficult.

(Flying on QF 085 from Brisbane to Cairns at 35,000 feet)

Maybe thinking is uncomfortable. Maybe we are biologically programmed to want to 'complete' our thinking as soon as possible. If you are playing roulette you watch the bobbing ball jitter around the number pockets hoping it will settle somewhere. Perhaps in thinking we want to come to some 'end point' or some conclusion as soon as possible. You are driving along a road in the early morning light. You see some strange shape on the road ahead of you. You feel extremely uncomfortable until you recognize that it is a truck with a loose tarpaulin. This urge to end thinking makes us seek as quick a judgement as possible. 'Maybe' and 'possibilities' are fine for design and creative thinking but distinctly uncomfortable in daily thinking. Certainty, right or wrong, has a high satisfaction value.

●━━━━━●

When you hear the word 'apple', do you think of a fruit or of a computer brand? It depends on the general context; on the particular context; and on the grammar. ('Do you like Apple?' or 'Do you like apples?') Many judgements are just as context specific, yet in practice we do not have time to specify the context, so we assume a 'common context', which may not be there at all. A person judged as incompetent may only have been incompetent in especially difficult circumstances. A person judged as 'kind' may only be kind when it suits that person. If you really enjoy helping other people does that make you selfish or altruistic – or both?

●━━━━━●

Solving problems is attractive. If you have a headache and you get rid of the headache the benefits are obvious and predictable. Removing a 'bad thing' will bring you back to normality. The 'design process' is not so satisfactory. The benefits have to be seen. There is no guarantee that the benefits will be delivered. You are dealing with the unknown. If you were sick and had to choose between a known remedy and a new one, which would you choose? If the known remedy worked well, why should you ever try a new remedy? Dealing with difficulties makes a lot of sense. Seeking to create new values only makes sense if you succeed.

●━━━━━●

Why are 'brands' so successful? Why do marketers seek so hard to create 'brands'? Because brands make judgement so much easier. Instead of having to try everything out you just trust the brand name: Kodak or Microsoft, for instance. The labelling is enough. Advertising is easier and more long term. Instead of having to advertise each product you promote the 'brand identity';

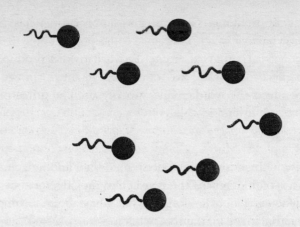

Surpetition

The toles are in a race against each other. This is classic competition.
One tole decides to choose its own direction. This could be
'surpetition'.

this then carries forward into the future to cover new products as well. If you have satisfied experience with a product then the brand allows you to carry that experience forward to other products. The positive effects of a brand are, of course, the mirror image of the negative effects of prejudice and stereotypes. The prime purpose of the brain is to simplify life.

●————●

There is an obvious interface between design and judgement. In the process of design itself there are constant judgements as to the best way to carry out the design: what fabric to use for the dress; what material to use for the roof; what music to play at the opening ceremony. At the end of the design process there are multiple judgements. Are the intended values delivered? Will the design be acceptable? Is implementation possible? How will critics react?

●————●

If you have a machine that randomly throws a number of shapes on to a surface, then an observer may notice an 'aesthetic' arrangement at some point and stop the process. A computer could do the random part of the operation very easily. This is no different from 'found art'. A computer could also be programmed with a few aesthetic rules and could then also 'choose' the most artistic arrangements. All this is no different from the classic view of evolution. There is some mechanism making random changes. Then 'survival' is the form of judgement that operates. Sometimes, the design process takes the form of multiple approaches, with the selection and development of the most promising.

●————●

Why have motor cars not changed very much for a hundred years? Probably because we have got so used to the current design that any radically new design would appear odd – just as the first Impressionist painters were treated as odd. No one dares introduce a new design because immediate sales of that design might be

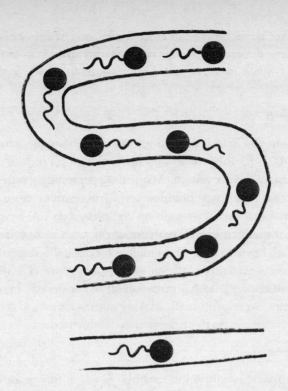

Complexity

Sometimes we do things in an unnecessarily complex way. Because this works we do not seek to change it. There may be a simpler and more direct way.

poor. Also, those buying a car are conscious of the resale value. For a new design the resale value is unknown. So the design process is stuck in an equilibrium state from which it dare not move away.

●━━━●

At one time the British motor industry was one of the strongest in the world. Today there is virtually no British motor industry. It may be the fault of the tax system. At one time personal income tax was so very high that it was pointless to pay executives more money. Instead the executives were given 'company cars'. At one time in the UK something like 66 per cent of car sales were to company fleets. Such fleets were brought mainly on price. So there was little consumer choice and so little consumer preference. There was no need to make continuous improvements in car design. In contrast, the Japanese were continually making improvements to get a share of the US market. So the British motor industry died.

●━━━●

Animals make very fine judgements. A white mouse can tell by smell whether another white mouse belongs to the same family grouping. Mice choose for mating other mice which have a different 'immune history'. Such mice have been exposed to a different environment and therefore are not likely to be of the same genetic family. There is some evidence that this may also be true of humans. If a man marries a woman who is not taking the contraceptive pill then he may not 'like' her when she starts taking the pill – and the other way around. Being on the pill is like a pseudo-pregnancy and animals want to be with their 'family grouping' under those conditions. All this is done by smell, without there being any conscious judgement at all.

●━━━●

Judgement is 'fit'. The key fits the lock. The door opens. What could be more satisfactory. We identify what something is: we know what to do with it; we know what to expect from it. There is a sort of 'click', almost like a key opening a lock. It is hardly surprising that judgement is such a necessary and such an attractive mental operation.

Some people seem to need certainty more than others. Their brains are perhaps more uncomfortable with ambiguity, doubt and uncertainty. Like a child that is upset because a regular meal is late, the brain wants 'closure' or identification.

The 'edge effect' means that something which everyone agrees is worth doing cannot be done if the very first step is unattractive – or not in the interests of those who have to take this step.

17

We know that progress depends on discovery, inventions, creation and design, but we have simply supposed that it happens anyway.

(Little Green island, off Shoal Point, Mackay, Queensland, Australia; tropical rain on the tin roof)

Judgement is designed to deal with the world as it is. We need to know what we are dealing with. Is it good to eat? Is this animal dangerous? How can this illness be cured? What will the economy do now? Is this behaviour legal? Is this person suitable for the job? That is why people like Socrates used to say 'knowledge is all'. If you know where you are and you have a road map then you know where to go. None of this is much use for design. Although design does happen we have never seriously developed a design culture. We know that progress depends on discovery, inventions, creation and design, but we have simply supposed that it happens anyway. It is supposed to happen by chance or through those few individuals who are motivated to move forward instead of simply adjusting to what is.

Judgement suggests that you have to show that something is bad or at least 'inadequate' before you seek to change it. Judgement implies that if something is not 'bad', then it must be good. And if it is good then there is no need to change it. Design has two functions: to make better what is adequate; and to deliver a value that has not yet been delivered. As technology advances there is more and more need to develop value concepts. Technology will support such concepts very well but technology alone will not develop value concepts.

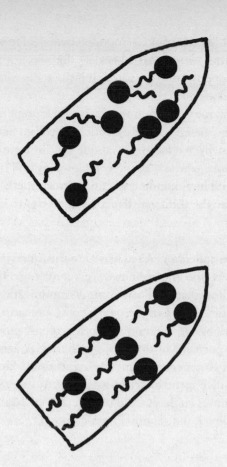

Wrong Direction

There is confusion everywhere. The ship's engines falter. The lights keep going out. The crew are demoralized. Then everything is put right. The crew are now organized and effective. Everything works. But the ship is still going in the wrong direction. Putting things right within a framework does not change that framework.

185

Imagine a traditional cook surrounded by lots of new ingredients. The ingredients are not used because they do not fit traditional recipes. The opportunity is wasted. It is the same with technology. Food alone does not create great dishes – great cooks do that. Technology alone only creates value up to a point – beyond that point only the design of value concepts will create new value. Books written by technologists about the future are often very banal. The uses to which the new technology will be put are not very exciting. The thinking that can deliver superb technology is not necessarily the thinking that is going to design new values.

●━━━━━━●

Is communication a value? Yes, if we are frustrated by lack of communication. Is freedom a value? Yes, if you are threatened by tyranny. But if you spend all your time communicating you may not have time to develop anything worth communicating. How much of the day does an average executive spend communicating? Probably 60 per cent of the time (in the USA managers spend an average of 40 per cent of the time in meetings). How much time does an executive spend in design thinking? At very most 5 per cent of the time, and even that would be exceptional. Maintenance and problem-solving is the general idiom in most organizations.

●━━━━━━●

Sophisticated satellite and other systems will tell the captain of a ship exactly where he is. Those systems will not tell him where he should be going. That may be a matter of following the orders laid down by the owner of the ship. That in turn may be a matter of routine or the result of information and negotiation. Somewhere in the system there is room for 'enterprise' and the design of new destinations and cargoes.

●━━━━━━●

We can teach judgement because we can teach comparison and identification. We have always felt that creativity and design cannot be taught. That was before we began to understand creativity as the behaviour of information in a self-organizing system. Creativity can be taught and so can design. But first we have to realize that these things are just as important as judgement.

●——————●

Your behaviour follows your judgements. Judgement determines where you go on holiday. Judgement determines who you choose as friends (and their judgement too). Judgement determines which restaurant you choose and what food you order when you get there. How often does our behaviour follow our designs?

●——————●

Animals do not redesign themselves or their lifestyles. They survive. They adapt. Evolution favours new random experiments. Could we not do the same? By and large we do – with moderate success. In doing so we are operating far below the potential that is offered by increased knowledge and technology. In the next millennium the gap is going to become greater. That is why it is necessary to increase our emphasis on design and design thinking to match our traditional emphasis on judgement.

●——————●

If too much change causes confusion and too little change produces stagnation, what is the right amount of change? Before answering that question it is useful to focus on 'the design of change'. Changes need to be designed so that they are easy to adopt, are acceptable, are motivating and deliver clear values. The design of anything must include the design of the implementation of that design. The perfect new idea that is unusable is useless. A ball on a sheet of foam rubber will follow the impression made by a thumb just in front of the ball. If the next step is easy and attractive, then that next step will be taken. Where change becomes confusing it has been badly designed.

●——————●

There is routine and there is change. In time the change will become a new routine. Access to routines is given by judgement. What standard situation do we identify? What is the standard response to this standard situation? This is an extremely effective system. If in this book I give the impression that there is anything wrong with that system, then that impression is unintended. My point is that it is an inadequate system by itself. A knife is excellent for its purpose but a knife and fork together allow more polite eating. Culturally we have allowed ourselves to be dominated by the judgement mode for two reasons. The first reason is that the mode is both practical and effective. The second reason is that the 'guardians' of our intellectual culture almost all come from the camp of analysis and judgement. The creative people are generally too creative to have time to sit in judgement on other people and their activities. We have evolved an education system that is quite excellent at resisting change.

•━━━━━━━•

Many years ago I ran a 'design' exercise for children in an educational publication. Youngsters were asked to design things like: 'a dog exercising machine'; 'how to build a house very quickly'; 'a sleep machine'; 'a new type of car wash', etc. This is very different from asking youngsters to draw a cottage with hollyhocks outside. Drawing is an ideal medium for children because they can express visually concepts that they would struggle to express verbally. I had six-year-olds showing 'negative feedback' systems without their ever understanding that term. The children loved putting together concepts to show how something could be done. For a dog exercising machine, many children had a sort of conveyor belt with a bone at the end to tempt the dog forward. One youngster had the dog pulling a small trolley on which was a car battery and a sort of prong. If the dog stopped the trolley would run into the dog, give the dog a shock and make the dog go on again. Instead of trying to get the dog to exercise, this young designer set out to prevent the dog from stopping. The advantage

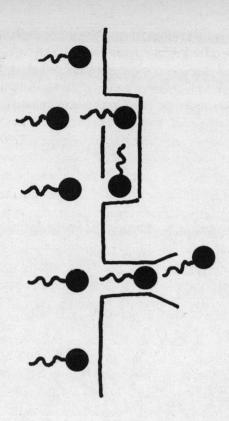

False Values

The opening seems to offer value but it is a false value and is not a way through the barrier. Some values only appear to be values.

of a drawing is that things have to be made explicit. It prevents the use of general words like 'encourage'. You have to show exactly how the encouragement is going to be delivered. The method works very well with children between the ages of five and twelve. After twelve youngsters seek to imitate what happens 'in real life'.

At each stage in civilization the guardians of culture are convinced that the best of all states has been achieved and that further progress will be limited to minor adjustments. Because of this thinking, the thinking becomes realistic – as a self-fulfilling prophecy.

Summary

At this point it may be useful to bring together the main threads of what has been considered so far. Most of the points will have become obvious, perhaps too obvious, to readers.

Traditional Thinking

Over the last two and a half thousand years we have developed, refined and used our classical thinking methods. These are marvellous, wonderful, excellent, effective and powerful. It is little wonder that we are tragically complacent about these methods. At the same time that they are so wonderful they are also inadequate. A carpenter may have the most wonderful saw in the world but without some method of sticking pieces of wood together the carpenter would only be doing half the job.

●———————●

Our traditional methods are concerned with 'what-is' thinking. What is this thing? What is this situation? What is the truth? This identification process allows us to use our experience and learning, and that of others, to apply standard solutions to standard situations.

●———————●

We have not been concerned with, nor have we put sufficient emphasis on, the other aspect of thinking, which is the 'what-can-be' type of thinking. This is the thinking that is concerned

193

with creativity, new ideas, new approaches and 'designing' the way forward. Excellent search methods will allow you to find a particular book in a library but such methods do not help you to write a new book. Perhaps we have been content to leave that side of thinking to individual talent, on the basis that such talent has indeed provided new ideas and inventions.

Analysis

At university level this is almost the key theme of intellectual effort: how can we analyse complex situations into their component parts so that we can understand the situation and perhaps apply a poultice of standard remedies.

●━━━━●

We can analyse problems and find the cause. We then seek to remove this cause. Sometimes we are successful, but when we cannot remove the cause we are paralysed, because such problems need the ability to design a way forward which leaves the cause in place.

●━━━━●

We are excellent at analysis but not nearly so good at design, because design needs a very different sort of thinking. How much time is spent at universities on 'design' as compared to 'analysis'?

Judgement

The purpose of analysis is to break things down so that we can judge and identify them. A doctor's skill depends on his or her ability to diagnose illness. This is a pure judgement process. Once the condition has been identified then the treatment is more or less standard. Once you know what you are dealing with then you

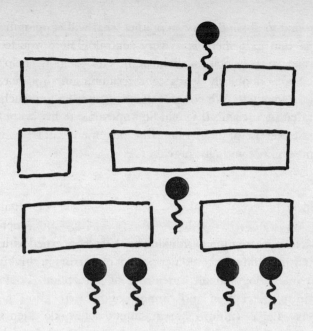

Achievement

There are barriers and ways through the barriers. Achievement means getting there. But you have to try – and to think constructively.

know what to do; and you can predict what will happen. Is it any surprise that judgement is so very central? There is judgement regarding laws, principles, behaviour, etc. Judgement feeds on difference and quickly leads to discrimination, injustice, persecution, wars, etc. We counter this by imposing another judgement: that of 'racism'. It would be impossible to live without the frequent exercise of judgement. But judgement can be tempered with possibilities and alternatives.

Logic

Almost all our attention to thinking has been concerned with logic. This is astonishing, since 90 per cent of our errors in thinking are not errors of logic at all but errors of perception. Logic does not control perception and cannot control perception (Godel's theorem). Logic within a system cannot determine the starting-points of the system. This hyper-emphasis on logic has had two disastrous effects. The first is that we have paid insufficient attention to 'perception' and the second is that we have the highly dangerous 'feeling' of being right – when we have selected the perceptions.

Being Right

If you feel you are 'right' then you may want to fight to the death to defend that feeling. Feeling right is an emotion, not just a logical state. We are taught that one of the highest forms of thinking is to defend a position logically. This is utter rubbish and dangerous rubbish too. If you select your information, choose your values, and restrict your perceptions, you can defend virtually any point of view. Much of the strife in the last millennium has arisen precisely from this 'feeling' of being right. Arrogance of the worst sort, both intellectual and behavioural, arises from this feeling of being right.

Truth

The driver of our thinking has been 'the search for the truth'. How can you do better than have 'the truth'? This is the essence of 'what-is' thinking. Leaving aside for the moment the consequent neglect of 'what-can-be' thinking, we can still see difficulties with the very concept of truth. Is there only one truth? In certain situations this is probably the case – but not in all situations. We extend the single-truth concept from occasions where it does apply to occasions where it does not apply. The conflicting witnesses of the black/white car in an accident both believed in their 'truth'. There are different sorts of truth: game truth, belief truth and experience truth. The single 'banner' of truth has been a very dangerous concept, driving people to heroic behaviour, as with martyrs, and to disastrous behaviour, as in the Inquisition.

Complacency

We have been far too smug and self-satisfied about our thinking habits. They have created a universe of discourse and consideration that cannot conceive of any other. If you live in France and speak French perfectly, how can you ever be aware of the deficiencies of that language? How can you conceive that there might be other languages? How can you accept that other languages may have advantages for certain purposes? How can anyone explain to you, in French, that French is not perfect? Our thinking habits see their own perfection in a limited universe of application and cannot consider the inadequacies of that universe. If you are content to play philosophical word games you cannot conceive that there is a huge world of 'practical thinking' which is totally different.

Problem-Solving

Arising directly from our complacency about our thinking habits and our lifestyle is our almost exclusive focus on 'problems'. Indeed, in much psychology any sort of thinking is called 'problem-solving'. Improvement means putting right faults and defects. In Japan, in contrast, improvement means making better what is already perfect. A problem is something that is 'wrong' and so we have to put it right. Business managers are obsessed with problem-solving, perhaps because they come across so many problems in their daily life. In practice, problem-solving is only a small part of thinking. Problems do have to be solved just as headaches do have to be treated. But you do not grow on a diet of aspirin salads. The creative, constructive and design aspects of thinking are even more important, but are largely neglected in favour of problem-solving. We do not even start to look at things unless they are problems. The result is that civilization is burdened with concepts and institutions which are marvellously inefficient but not yet problematic enough to attract 'thinking attention'.

Not Good Enough

Our obsession with faults and problems means that you have to prove something to be incorrect or 'bad' for it to be changed. There is probably no subject in the crowded educational curriculum which is bad, harmful or not worth teaching. Everything there has a value. It is only when we look at the vastly more important subjects which are excluded because of the full curriculum that we can see that the 'good' is not good enough. Subjects like 'thinking', 'operacy' and 'value creation in society' are far more important than the majority of subjects now on the curriculum. In exactly the same way, our traditional thinking habits are not 'bad': they are excellent, but not good enough, in the sense that

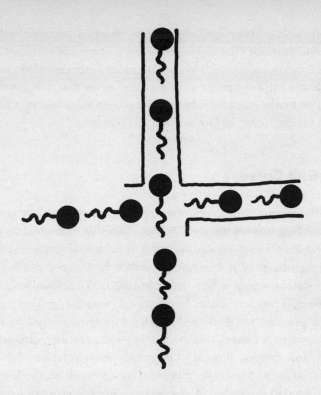

The Next Step

The direction in which a tole is swimming will determine the direction of the 'next step'. Once a tole enters a channel the next step is even more determined. Freedom to choose is only there when we choose to exercise it. Mostly our next steps are determined by where we are.

they are not complete and leave out the design aspects of thinking. We tend to insist that change can only come about if you first prove the existing method to be wrong. This automatically prevents us making improvements in the many areas that are good but could be made very much better. The front left wheel of a motor car is excellent but, by itself, not good enough.

The Salt Curve

This dangerous fault arises directly from our judgement system. If something is good then surely more is better. If communication is good then more communication is better. If globalization is good then more of it is better. No salt is bad. Some salt is good. More salt, however, is not better but bad. We acknowledge this and we talk vaguely about 'moderation' and the 'golden mean', but in practice we disregard it. Development is good so more development is better. Technology is good so more technology is better. Information is good so more information is better. A PhD scholar wanting to access references to my work on the Internet would need to spend thirty working years, spending just one minute on each reference. Fast planes are good, so faster planes are better. Yet the supersonic Concorde has not had successors and is not a commercial success.

Argument

This arises directly from judgement, identification, truth and the 'what-is' system. One party insists that the situation is A and the other party insists either that it is 'not A' or that it is B. The argument goes back and forth as in an adversarial court of law. The prosecution insists on the guilt of the defendant and the defence insists on his innocence. This is meant to explore the subject – but it does not, for obvious reasons. If the defence lawyer thinks of a point which actually favours the prosecution, that point is never going to be advanced. The primitive and crude nature of the argument system is shown up very clearly in contrast with the parallel thinking of the very simple Six Hats method. In this method every thinker at any moment is looking in the same direction. The direction can be changed (hence the six hats). Meetings take only a quarter or even one tenth of the usual time. Meetings are far more productive. Problems that could not be solved are solved. Those who have become familiar with the method look back with wonder at the inefficiency of traditional argument.

Perception

There used to be a saying in the computer world of GIGO: which meant, 'garbage in – garbage out'. The logic of the computer would be working flawlessly, but if you put in rubbish you got rubbish out. It is the same with human logic. If the starting perceptions are faulty or inadequate then flawless logic will produce absurd answers. But, much more dangerously, we will believe those answers to be valid. We have neglected the vitally important area of perception, because logicians only worked with fixed starting concepts. We have neglected perception because we did not know how to deal with it. Our traditional habits of thinking are completely useless when it comes to perception. Perception works in a self-organizing information system, logic works in an externally organized system: two completely different information universes. All my work started from consideration of self-organizing information systems like the nerve networks in the brain. Logic works with truth and deduction. Perception works with possibilities, alternatives and provocations. Applying logic to perception is like trying to sculpt with water (not ice). There is nothing to get hold of – yet it is there.

Our approach to perception has to be very different. One approach is to design simple attention-directing tools. These are incredibly simple but very powerful. Thirty youngsters liked the idea of being paid to go to school. They were asked to use the PMI attention-directing tool, and as a result of that simple perceptual scan twenty-nine out of the thirty completely changed their minds. There was no argument or discussion: just a broadening of perception. The same tools taught to totally illiterate workers at the bottom of a platinum mine in South Africa reduced disputes from two hundred and ten a month to just four. Such methods are so simple and there is so much experience with them across cultures, ages and abilities, that any education system that does not put them into every school is failing in its duty.

Possibility

This is a key part of thinking. It is the very basis of science, along with the hypothesis. Without the hypothesis there is no science. It is the very basis of technology with vision. Unless we can imagine something we cannot undertake to achieve it. Our traditional thinking does acknowledge the importance of hypotheses but does very little about them. This is because logic has to move from one certainty to another. Possibilities are the very opposite of certainty. Furthermore possibilities cannot be produced by analysis – they require a creative and design effort.

Creativity

Our traditional thinking habits ignore creativity completely. Creativity is regarded as a mystical talent that some people have and that produces creative results. It is considered beyond analysis and incapable of being harnessed. This is complete nonsense. Creativity arises from the perfectly logical behaviour in a self-organizing

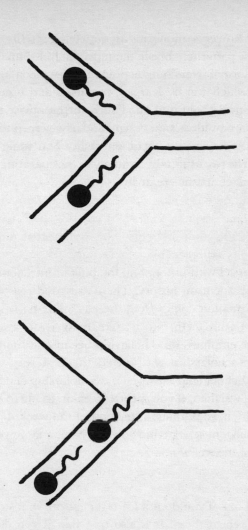

Choice of Direction

Too often we feel we have to choose either/or. Sometimes this is the case (as in going for a walk). But we can also choose to go in different directions at the same time (as in investing).

system, which necessarily forms asymmetric patterns. There is a need to cross patterns – hence the term 'lateral thinking'. There are various formal techniques of doing this (provocation, random entry, etc.) which can be learned, practised and used. There is nothing mystical about it at all. This is the creativity involved in new concepts, new ideas, new designs and new perceptions. Artistic creativity also requires aesthetic sensibility and some emotional resonance. The two aspects of creativity need separating, otherwise we only think of artistic creativity.

History

We are obsessed with history and the bulk of intellectual effort at universities is spent on history. There are good reasons for this. All our information comes from the past. The past is there and you can 'get your teeth into it'. Creativity is not essential. We place a huge emphasis on scholarship because at the time of the Renaissance scholarship was indeed the best way to get new knowledge. Scholarship shows effort. Scholarship can be assessed and, almost, weighed. If you spent a week on trying to have a new idea you may have nothing at the end of the week. If you spend a week on diligent scholarship you will have a large pile of notes at the end of the week.

●——————●

We are told that if you do not learn the lessons of history you are doomed to repeat them. It is also true that if you do learn the lessons of history you are doomed to be trapped by them!

●——————●

There is nothing wrong with history except the huge overemphasis on history. If we had spent as much time on 'design' as we spend on history, the world would be a very different place. Water is essential for life – but you can also drown in water.

Information

A large pile of bricks does not build a house. A sack of flour does not bake a cake. Information has a high value. Information can provide you with answers you could not work out for yourself. Information can provide the ingredients for your new design. Information on its own will not do all your thinking for you. The information age is over. We can now get all the information we want. Information is no longer the bottleneck. Thinking is the new bottleneck. How do we get value from information? This is a design process. Billions are spent on information technology. How much is spent on better thinking? Virtually nothing.

Communication

Isolation is a bad thing so communication is a good thing. So more communication must be better. So more and more communication must be even better. The stage has already been reached where some people are so overburdened with communication that they cannot do much else except cope with the communication. The telephone was an obvious blessing, but it also meant that you did not have to make friends with your neighbours because you could have friends at a distance. Communication is not a substitute for thinking. A poor idea shouted very loudly is still a poor idea. You only have to look at some Internet chat rooms to appreciate this.

Technology

There is a hidden hope that somehow technology will solve problems. This is partly true. Sophisticated and powerful weapons may make all wars obsolete. Medical advances may make us live longer and healthier lives. Computers can run, control and even design systems for us. Computer matching can find us mates. The isolation of certain 'bonding' chemicals may lock us into a lifetime mutual obsession with a mate – just as happens with the prairie vole. On the whole, however, technology is already far in advance of the 'value concepts' we have designed. Technology will support our value concepts – but it will not provide value. The emphasis now needs to be on the 'design' of value concept. Technology companies are completely unaware of this.

Design

Design is almost the opposite of judgement. Judgement is attending to what is there. Design is seeking to bring about something that is not yet there. At different points, judgement and analysis do come into the design process, but the thrust and framework of design thinking is very different. You can analyse the factors needed to invent a new game – but you still have to design the game. The purpose of design is to bring together different things in order to deliver value. If there is no value there is no design. If the only value is the self-indulgence of the designer, then there is no design either. Design is the opposite of complacency and being too happy with things the way they are. Creativity feeds into design. A design may be a new way of putting together well-known things. A design may also involve new concepts. Design can be applied to everything we do, think or feel. We may seek to design new types of capital; we may seek to design a better form of democracy; we may seek to redesign the legal system. Anything can be designed or redesigned. Design is very much more than just problem-solving.

Value

Value is to design as truth is to logic. Logic seeks to proceed from truth to truth. Design seeks to proceed from value to value. The many aspects of value will be described in later pages. There may

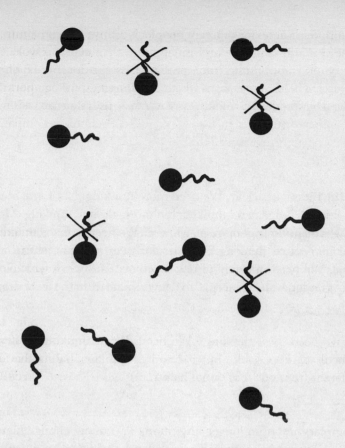

Remove the Bad

We believe that if we identify the 'bad' and remove it then all will be well. So we eliminate the toles that are swimming in a 'bad' direction. This does not do very much to get the other toles swimming in the right direction.

207

be different values for different people. Negative values have to be kept in mind. Design is very much more than classical synthesis, where thesis and antithesis are combined. Design does not exist until it exists. The elements from which the design is put together may indeed be standard elements – just as music uses standard notes.

So . . .

So the message is clear. We need more thinking. Not more of the traditional 'judgement' thinking but more 'design' thinking. More of 'what-can-be', not more of 'what-is'. We need to teach thinking, and perceptual thinking in particular (it is possible, cheap and easy). We need not only to develop more and more technology but to design 'value concepts' to deliver value from the technology.

•———•

So we need 'new thinking'. We need design thinking. It is not difficult or impossible, but it requires thinking habits that are different from our traditional habits.

•———•

Complacency is no longer an option. Too many change factors have been set in motion. They all have their own momentum. Sitting still does not mean the world around will also sit still. Keeping up is a choice. Moving ahead is an even better choice.

•———•

Some of the characteristics of the new thinking are explored in the following pages.

PART TWO
Design

Design, Constructive and Creative Thinking

Design thinking is very different from traditional judgement thinking. For judgement thinking the desired output is truth, or apparent truth. For design thinking the output is value.

For logical thinking, certainty is essential. For design thinking, possibility is essential.

Logical thinking likes to work with facts. Design thinking has to work with perception.

The three most important things in design thinking are: perception, possibility and practicality (the three Ps).

Traditional thinking is based on analysis, judgement and logic. Design thinking is far more different than most people realize. Design is not simply a different purpose to which traditional thinking can be applied just as it is applied to any other purpose. This is an unfortunate mistake made by every educational establishment throughout the world. The serious result of this mistake is that no attempt is made to teach design thinking. Even less effort is made to teach creative thinking, which is a key component of design thinking. This is also because creativity is still, quaintly, regarded as a mystical gift which cannot be taught.

As an appendix to this work, I shall give an outline of frameworks and programmes which are used very successfully by top executives in some of the world's largest corporations, by the public services, in schools and with children as young as four-years-olds (some programmes). These will only be covered in outline since it would be unfair to repeat here what many readers will already know.

In the following pages I intend to set out some new considerations which have not appeared in any previous work of mine.

(1.33 a.m. UK time; on Qantas QF 1 flying in to London; bumpy)

Movement Vs. Judgement

'Po the factory should be downstream of itself.' The word 'po' is a word I invented to indicate 'provocative operation'. There was a need in language to indicate that something was not meant to be 'true' but was intended as a provocation. The human brain (like any self-organizing system) needs provocation. Language never provided a means for provocation because language is about 'what-is' and not about 'what-can-be'. Provocation is one of the key operations of lateral thinking.

Judgement would immediately dismiss the idea of a factory being downstream of itself as being totally ridiculous.

Movement is a very different mental operation from judgement. Judgement is part of what I have called 'rock logic', which is the logic of unchangeable identity and truth. Movement is part of 'water logic', where flow is the main value. Judgement is concerned with 'is' and 'is not': 'this fits' and 'this does not fit'. Movement is concerned with 'to': 'what does this lead to'; 'what does this flow to'.

We imagine the factory downstream of itself. It would get its own pollution. The same effect could be produced if the factory input had to be placed downstream of its own output.

Movement is a distinct mental operation and not just an absence of judgement. Movement is moving from one idea to another. Movement is moving from an idea to a concept or from a concept

212

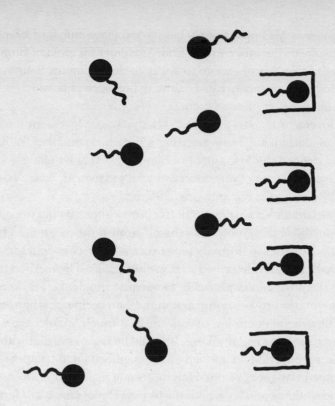

Boxes

Once we have identified something and placed it in its 'box', then we do not need to think further about it. We know what it is. Judgement is an effort to place everything in its right box.

to an idea. Movement is moving from a concept to a broader concept – or the other way round. Movement is moving from an idea to value or from value to a way of delivering the value.

Movement is much, much more than association, which is but one small aspect of movement.

Movement is a key part of design thinking. Movement is a key part of all thinking. How amazing it is then, to find that we have never defined this key aspect of human thinking let alone taught it. This is because of our obsession with judgement, which has so totally dominated our thinking culture.

The lateral-thinking technique of provocation lays out some formal methods of getting 'movement' from a provocation. These methods can be used formally, systematically and deliberately. Such methods are fully described in my other books. The method used with the provocation above is 'moment to moment'. This means imagining the provocation in action and then 'seeing what happens'.

The general operation of movement is much broader than the specific use in lateral thinking. It would be fair to say that without some mental skill in movement, design would be impossible. Talented designers instinctively use some aspects of movement. Understanding and laying out the process of movement in a formal manner greatly enhances the power of this instinctive use and makes it available to those who do not do it instinctively.

How absurd and arrogant of us to have believed that judgement was the only valid response to an idea.

An idea might be worthless or dangerous in itself, but with the skill of movement we can move on from the worthless idea to a better idea. Often we do this by extracting the concept and then finding a better way to deliver the concept.

It has not been my intention in this brief focus on 'movement' to lay out its full nature and formal ways of doing it. I have merely sought to indicate why our exclusive reliance (and teaching) of judgement is so limited and inadequate.

As we move from analysing the past to designing the future we are going to need to develop the mental operation of 'movement'.

Value Solving

(Little Green Island, Mackay)

In my book *Surpetition* I suggested the word 'valufacture' to indicate the creation of value. In a sense anything we do is intended to create some value – either for the moment or more long term. With valufacture the emphasis is directly on value in the first place. Then we consider means of delivering that value.

When we are solving a problem or seeking to achieve some task we usually work backwards. We think of a broad general approach. Then we work back to a concept. Finally we seek an idea which will link up with our capabilities at the moment. What can we actually do?

In 'value solving' we can do the same for values. You need to be very specific about the value to be achieved. Then you work backwards to find a way of delivering the desired value.

This working backward in 'value solving' is not quite the same as designing forward to deliver the value. Providing the value becomes a 'task'; the absence of the value forms a 'problem'; so we set about problem-solving. This method is useful, but less powerful than the design method because at best it will produce standard solutions.

There is nothing wrong with standard solutions and most of the time this is the most practical and most reliable way of doing anything. Repeating standards solutions endlessly is not, however, going to provide better solutions. The thinking involved in 'getting by' is not the same as the thinking involved in 'doing better'.

How do you make a worker happy? Give him more money might be a standard solution. The design of better working conditions; better working relations; more involvement in the design of the work; more leisure time; and training for promotion might be less standard approaches.

Standard solutions allow quick thinking. Quick thinking is not in itself a virtue unless you are about to be involved in a car accident. Top-speed decisions do have the value of 'firm decisions' but rarely have the value of 'best decisions'.

Producing Ideas

There are many ways of 'producing ideas'. Four of them are considered here. When you need an idea, you need an idea. You have to 'produce' an idea. How do you do it?

The Concept Base

If you can define the concept, then you can look around for ways of carrying out that concept. If you define the concepts as 'fast food', then you look around for examples of fast food: hamburgers, pizzas, chicken, etc. Then you define another concept: 'food which is self-contained'. This may lead on to ideas like sandwiches, pasta, pancakes, soups, etc. Some of these are already being used as 'fast foods'. Working downwards from a concept to idea will usually produce ideas. The ideas may not be highly original, because the process is really a 'search process'. We search through our repertoire under that concept heading.

We may move from concept to idea and then up to another concept and down to another idea. It is rather like looking through a telephone directory to find all the names listed under the letter 'D'. Under 'D' you find a name like 'DiCaprio'. This sounds Italian so now you pursue the Italian 'concept' and find examples of Italian names.

Most of the time our thinking produces ideas in exactly this way. That is why concepts are so important a part of thinking.

The 'Concept Fan' method in lateral thinking does this in a systematic way, working through several levels of concept to open up a multitude of alternative ideas.

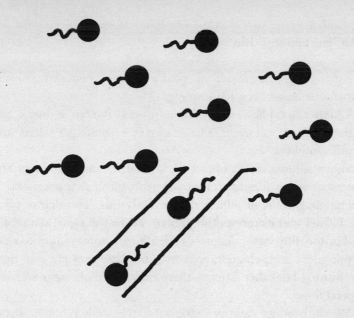

Technology as Value

The toles are all swimming in one direction. Technology provides a
swift channel. But is it in the right direction? Technology can provide
the means but this is not the same as value.

The 'Something' Method

What is round, flat, made of meat and eaten between two half buns? The answer is a hamburger.

Children's riddles follow this approach. 'What is black and white and "red" all over?' The answer is a newspaper – 'red' and 'read' sound the same.

When we identify an object we lay out the characteristics and then search our files for something with those characteristics. A doctor diagnosing an illness does exactly this. The doctor takes the history and examines the patient. From the signs, symptoms and history the doctor diagnoses the 'illness'. Some conditions like peptic ulcer and schizophrenia may be diagnoses entirely from the history. For other illnesses there may be visible signs and also special tests.

We can produce ideas by laying out all the needed characteristics of the idea. This array of characteristics will often produce specific ideas.

We say to ourselves: 'I need "something" with the following characteristics . . .' I need something which is: small, can transport single people and requires no external power. The ideas that come to mind almost immediately are: bicycle, skates, skateboard and even skis.

So we list the characteristics of the 'something' we need and then we find we have produced a specific thing.

Lateral Thinking

The specific processes of lateral thinking can be used deliberately to produce ideas. For instance we need a new idea for fast food and we use the Random Word technique. The random word is 'bed'. Through a quick association with sex, we might get oysters, which are supposed to be an aphrodisiac (only for men, who might be short of zinc if overactive). So the idea is for an oyster bar, which serves oysters cooked in various ways or natural.

Other techniques of lateral thinking, such as provocation, can also serve to generate ideas.

Borrow or Transfer

'Instant glue' is very powerful and sticks to your skin if you are not careful. So surgeons borrowed the idea and use a special type of instant glue to close operation openings – instead of sewing up the opening. Attempts have been made to use the way a dolphin glides through the water in designing the hull of a racing yacht.

Natural processes may be borrowed. Processes used in other industries can also be transferred. The Russians had a sort of assembly-line process for their operations on the human cornea to correct short-sightedness.

You take a process which seems vaguely likely to be relevant and then you see how well it fits. Usually the concept will work but the details have to be changed.

Each of the above processes will 'produce' an idea by bringing to mind an already existing idea. This can be valuable because the idea may never have been considered in this new context.

Modification, Change and Challenge

Here we take an existing idea and then seek to change it. One simple way to change an existing idea is to use the 'challenge' process of lateral thinking. We challenge why some element needs to be there at all, or needs to be done in that particular way. Why do all telephone kiosks in a row have to charge the same price? If we make one of them very expensive then that kiosk is very likely to be empty because no one would want to use it – and even if they did use it they would be very brief. The value is that if you really needed to make an urgent call you could now do so – and pay the high price for this benefit.

It is said that in an old wooden boat, none of the wood is part of the original boat. One piece is changed and then another. The boat keeps its exact shape but eventually all the wood has been replaced. So an idea may be changed again and again until there is no resemblance to the original idea (unlike the boat, in that the form changes, but like the boat in the sense of continued changes).

Why does each match in a box have to have a combustible head? Maybe some matches would just be sticks with no heads, and the box would contain a few paper tubes so that the matches could be joined together; there are times when you need a longer match or a longer-burning match. In fact the matches could still all have heads – but there would be some joining tubes as well in the box (joining the matches end to end).

Combination

This is a standard way of producing a new idea. Take two different things and seek to put them together. Put a car and a boat together and you get an amphibian vehicle. Put a ladder and a wheelbarrow together and you get a better way of carrying a ladder and a trolley for carrying things. Put a frying-pan and a grill together and you can turn the frying-pan upside down to go more easily under the grill. Put vehicle insurance and registration tax together and the insurance company becomes responsible for collecting the tax. Put chopsticks and a spoon together and you get a small 'spoon head' that can be picked up by inserting the chopsticks in slots.

Put a fax machine, a telephone and a printer together and you get a widely available machine.

The very combination might require creative thinking and the further development of the starting idea might require further creative thinking.

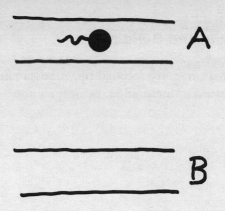

Criticism

If the tole is swimming in channel A we can argue that it should be in channel B. If the tole was swimming in channel B we could then argue that it should be in channel A. Criticism is much easier and of much less value than we believe.

Constructing and Building

Sometimes it is necessary to build up, construct or assemble an idea. This process is discussed in the next section.

Design Operations (Dops)

Our normal logic is 'rock logic', or the logic of identity: 'What is this?' Design requires a different sort of logic: 'water logic'. Water logic involves 'flow'. Rock logic is concerned with whether something 'is' or 'is not' a particular known category or thing. The operating term in water logic is 'to': 'What does this flow to?'

This 'flow' aspect of water logic and design thinking is not random. There is some structure for the flow from one idea to another. There is some mental operation which affects the flow.

In traditional thinking there are formal operations like 'analysis', whereby we give ourselves the operating instruction to seek to break something down into its component parts. Another formal operation is 'judgement': comparison with some proposed item, category, principle or law. Another operation might be 'inference': 'If these things are true, what follows, what can we infer?'

In addition to using these same operations, design thinking also has its own operations. Some of these are listed here. The list is not comprehensive.

It is not expected that the term 'DOP' will enter common usage but it stands conveniently for 'Design Operation'. In what follows, the dops are numbered to provide a convenient reference code.

Move up to a Broader Concept (dop 1)

Concepts are the key to design thinking. Often, a design starts out with a very broad concept. Concepts are full of 'potential'. From a concept we can 'flow' in many directions. It is almost impossible to move from one detail or one idea to another without going back to the concept. The search for the underlying concept (operating concept) is a key part of lateral thinking. 'What is the operating concept here?' So dop 1 is the intention or effort to move up to a broader concept. The move may be from an idea to a concept or from a concept to a broader concept. A telephone rings when there is a call. What is the concept? A means of attracting attention. How else might we do this? There might be a blinking light. A practical idea might be to have a phone which can be switched between 'ring' and 'light' as you wish. The light might even blink for a few moments and then continue as a 'ring' if the phone is not answered.

Moving up to a concept is very powerful – but seldom done because people are suspicious of the 'vagueness' of concepts.

Moving Down to an Idea or Concept (dop 2)

Once we have the concept we can find other ways of carrying it out (dop 2). The concept of the dial buttons on a phone is 'to identity' the number to be called. We do a 'dop 2' and ask how else could we do this? There might just be one number to a central voice-recognition computer and you would just speak the number or give the person's name.

Eventually, every concept needs to be brought down to a practical idea. There is, however, no rush to do this. You can work at the concept level for quite a while before having to come down to an idea.

Parallels and Alternatives (dop 3)

Again this is a key operation in design thinking. How else could we do this? What are the alternatives here? The alternatives seek to carry out the same function; to have the same purpose; or deliver the same value. Whenever we seek alternatives there is always a background 'concept' in our mind. Otherwise the alternative would be random. Perhaps the first way of doing something is too expensive, or illegal, or unacceptable. So we want to keep the same concept but find another way of putting it into practice. The flashing light on the phone is an alternative to a ringing sound. A further alternative would be to have the light instead of the sound if the phone 'sensed' that someone was near by.

Alternatives are very much part of the 'possibility' component of design thinking. There may be alternative ideas but there may also be alternative concepts and alternative values. All these are generated as 'possibilities'. Whether these possibilities are valuable, attractive, practical or even do-able has to be assessed later. There should be no attempt to reject alternatives on the basis that they do not seem practical at first glance. An impractical idea can often lead to a very practical one.

Factor Scan (dop 4)

This is an essential starting-point in design thinking. What factors do we have to keep in mind. One of the key attention-directing tools in the school programme (CoRT) or the business programme (DATT) is CAF: Consider All Factors.

Instead of focusing on the current idea or even the purpose of the design, we scan around to see what 'factors' need to be considered. In designing a chair, such factors as comfort, strength, appearance, robustness, cost and ease of manufacture might all need to be considered.

These various factors may be built into the design brief. Sometimes they may be specific requirements. At other times the factors simply need to be considered. For example, sharp corners on a chair would not be suitable if there might be toddlers around. Should the factor that some people like to tilt back in their chair be taken into account? Possibly.

Challenge (dop 5)

This is also one of the basic operations of lateral thinking. Challenge is easy to describe but much less easy to apply. We are very used to focusing on defects and seeking to put them right. With challenge we focus on something which is not a defect at all. We acknowledge that it may be the best way to do something – and may indeed be the only way. Nevertheless we set out to challenge 'uniqueness'. Is this the only way to do it? We can also challenge 'necessity'. Do we really need to do this at all? The outcome of a challenge is either a different way of doing it (or a different approach) or dropping the item completely.

Change (dop 6)

This is the opposite of complacency. The 'self-instruction' is to make a change. The change should be substantial and not just a minor modification. The direction of change is not indicated, but could be specified. In general, dop 6 implies dissatisfaction and the beginning of a search for other possibilities. There is no need to give any reason for the requested change – even to yourself. It is not a matter of changing something because that something is not practical or is too expensive. In a sense it is 'change for the sake of change'. The purpose of the change is to open up new possibilities and to prevent 'bedding down' in too early a complacency. There is an obvious overlap between 'challenge' and 'change'. On the whole 'challenge' is more fundamental. The search for alternative ideas or concepts follows both operations.

Modify (dop 7)

This is a lesser version of 'change'. The instruction is to keep the central idea or concept but to modify it. The direction of modification would usually be made explicit. The idea might need to be made more practical; cheaper to implement; more acceptable to the local culture; more suitable for existing mechanisms, etc. Modifications might range from minor ones to ones so major that the whole idea seems changed.

Modification can be used early in the design process as an opening-up procedure. Modification can also be used later in the process to make the idea more usable and more valuable.

It is extremely unlikely that any idea will be so perfect when first thought of that no further modification will be needed.

Develop (dop 8)

The difference between 'modify' and 'develop' is that develop is more fundamental. As we develop an idea we might find it changing into a new idea. Develop also means 'fleshing out' an idea so that more detail is given. In short, 'develop' means 'take this idea further'. It also means: 'work with this idea'.

'Develop' is the opposite of 'change' or 'challenge' or even 'parallel'. In all these operations we seek to move away from the current idea. With 'develop' we stay with the current idea and work on it.

In practice, we could distinguish between 'develop this idea' and, 'develop this line of thought'. Both imply staying with something and working on it.

Combine (dop 9)

This is a fairly obvious and basic operation. There are two, or more, things which we try to bring together. You may seek to combine the portability of a laptop computer with the power of a desktop. Manufacturers are doing quite a good job of that. You may want to combine the full loads of charter flights with the regular timetable of scheduled flights. You may want to combine the high yield of junk bonds with the security of government bonds. There are many attempts to combine opposites. Not many of them are successful.

As a design intention, and process, combination is well worth trying. The design process does not guarantee an outcome.

Pick Out (dop 10)

One of the processes of 'movement' in lateral thinking is to 'pick out' or extract some feature, concept or principle from the provocation. We then ignore the rest and just work with what we have picked out.

Even the most unlikely idea may contain some feature that has value. We can jettison the idea but keep the value of that feature. Picking out a concept is very similar to dop 1. The intention, however, is to pick 'something' out. This something may turn out to be a concept. If we try hard enough to find value we become better at finding value.

There is never an obligation to use a 'whole idea'. We are free to take whatever part we like of the idea.

Context (dop 11)

At first glance this operation may seem similar to consideration of the factors (dop 4). The difference is that the factors are involved in the design itself whereas context looks at the surroundings of the design need. What is the time scale? What are the cost limits? What is the design supposed to achieve? How radical a design is expected or acceptable? Who is going to assess the design? For how many years is the design going to have to last? Who else is competing? Where is the design going to be placed? etc., etc. Some aspects, such as cost, are both factors and part of the context.

We very rarely have a 'pure' design situation where the best design would be acceptable. The context usually plays a large part in the acceptance of the design.

Set and Solve (dop 12)

This is really two operations but they usually go together. We set a task. We set a problem. We ask a question. We seek improvement in a defined direction. Then we set about achieving the task, solving the problem, etc. The verbal definition of the task needs to be precise – even if the contents are broad: 'We need some way of getting water to the top of the hill'; 'We need to turn wind power into energy'; 'I want you to suggest a way of rewarding people who turn up new ideas.'

It has long been suggested that 'defining the problem' is almost as important as solving the problem. This applies to any sort of thinking task that we set for ourselves.

Once we have 'set' the task we go about 'solving' it. This is no different from any other sort of problem-solving. We work through concepts and standard approaches. We try creative approaches. We may or may not solve the problem. We may even have to restate the problem: 'Can we catch the water that falls on the top of the hill?'

Setting a problem or task is not much different from posing a question.

Provocation (dop 13)

Normally, we do not say something unless there is a reason for saying it. With 'provocation' there may not be a reason for saying something until after it has been said.

In any self-organizing information system (like the human brain) there is a mathematical need for 'provocation' in order to jerk us out of a local equilibrium.

The word 'po' was invented by me to indicate a 'Provocative Operation'. 'Po cars should have square wheels' seems utterly absurd from a traditional engineering point of view. In fact, the provocation leads to the concept of suspension that acts in anticipation of need.

There are formal ways of setting up provocations (like reversal). There are formal ways of getting 'movement' from provocations. These require more thorough explanation than I have space for here. The various techniques of lateral thinking merit proper attention and are described in some of my other books (see the Appendix).

Strengthen (dop 14)

An idea can be strengthened in two ways. One way is to remove the faults and weaknesses. The other way is to build up the strong points of the idea. This operation covers both aspects.

Fault correction is similar to problem-solving and will involve modification of the idea.

In general, we are less likely to seek to enhance the strength of an idea than to remove its faults. Yet building on the strength of an idea may be even more valuable.

Too many ideas are presented in a weak form, far below the potential of the idea, because no one has made any effort to strengthen the idea. There is no reason to suppose that the first version of an idea is the most powerful.

Make Practical (dop 15)

This is a most important operation, because unless an idea can be made practical that idea cannot deliver value. Since the purpose of design is to deliver value, making something practical is rather important.

There are a whole number of different way in which an idea can be made practical: cost, acceptance, using existing mechanisms, etc., etc.

What is indicated by dop 15 is the clear intention to make the idea practical – in whatever aspects are needed for that idea. The focus of the thinking shifts from conceiving new ideas to making an existing idea more practical. This attempt may succeed or it may not.

Making something more practical may require a trade-off in values. Simplifying an idea may make it less powerful. Lowering the cost may lower the value.

Analysis (dop 16)

Traditional analysis can be used at many stages in the design process. Analysis means sorting out functions, needs and values. Matters are analysed into their component parts so they can be considered and dealt with more directly.

There may also be a need to analyse existing approaches in order to see how they work and in order to design a better approach.

Divide Up (dop 17)

We can divide up a design task into sub-tasks so that we can deal more easily with each sub-task. The process is very different from analysis, which seeks out the true component elements. 'Dividing up' is only for our own convenience. We can divide something up into parts which are totally arbitrary. There is no pretence that we are discovering the true constituents. In designing a new cup we could divide the task up as follows: rim, handle, bowl, fit on saucer, decoration, interior, etc.

Dividing up is for the sake of attention and also action. The areas separated out may well overlap and what is decided in one area may affect others.

You can look at a building from many angles. You know it is a single building but the different focuses allow you to do more than you could have done with only one focus.

The danger is always that parts dealt with in isolation may not integrate as a final whole.

Value Scan (dop 18)

This is the most important operation of all. What are the values? What values does this design deliver? The purpose of any design is to deliver value. If there are no values, then there is no design.

The 'value scan' should be as broad as possible and must include negative values as well as positive values. Various scanning 'frames' could be used, such as PMI (from the DATT programme) or the parallel thinking of the Six Hats.

What is important is that the scan should be systematic. A haphazard scan is very likely to leave out important considerations. Less obvious values such as 'convenience', 'hassle' and 'simplicity' should not be ignored.

A value scan is not necessarily a final assessment. Following the value scan, further work can be done on the idea to strengthen it or to modify it in the light of what the value scan has revealed.

Fit (dop 19)

The term 'fit' is used in its broadest sense. Does this design 'fit' the design brief? Does this design 'fit' the context? Does this design 'fit' available resources (money, management, time, etc.). Does this design 'fit' this particular organization? Does this design 'fit' the local culture? Does this design 'fit' the people who are going to have to work with it and live with it?

Although 'fit' is a sort of judgement, it is much more relative. 'Fit' refers to a very particular situation, whereas judgement tends to deal in absolutes. Judgement might declare that something is 'too expensive'. 'Fit' might find that it is indeed expensive but fits the need for ostentation. 'Fit' refers to the idiosyncrasies of people and situations. In one situation a peculiarity of history might make a design unacceptable although the design is excellent in itself and may have won awards elsewhere. An example was the choice of the name 'Nova' for a car: unfortunately in South America it suggested '*No va*' – meaning that the car would not go.

'Fit' is indeed a very broad term but it is as essential to design thinking as is 'value'. If the design is full of value but there is no 'fit', then all that value is useless because it cannot be delivered. Design is about delivered value.

Random Entry (dop 20)

This is another very specific technique from lateral thinking. The use of this technique is particularly valuable in three situations.

It is useful in green-field situations, where you are asked to design from nothing. There is no existing starting-point. There is nothing to work with or to work against. The random-entry technique will provide several possible starting-points.

The technique is useful when ideas seem stuck, when it does not seem possible to find a really different approach. The thinking keeps coming back to the same ideas again and again. The random-entry technique can serve to open up new possibilities.

The technique is also useful in 'stagnant' situations where all previous thinking on the subject has stayed within the same confines. There seems to be no way out of these confines. The random-entry can provide 'out of the box' ideas.

As explained earlier in this book, the random-entry technique may seem totally illogical but is actually logical in a 'patterning system' where entry from the periphery can open up paths which cannot be accessed from the centre.

The deliberate use of the random-entry technique is a powerful source of new starting-points.

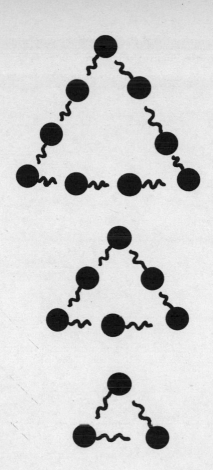

Evolution

Things evolve to get better and better – but usually in the same
direction. A stage is reached where further evolution may not be
possible. The top triangle arrangement of toles evolves to become
simpler and simpler but reaches a final form which cannot evolve
further.

Design Values (devs)

As with the 'design operations', there is no suggestion that the 'design values' be permanently labelled as devs. The notation is there for convenience only.

The 'design values' listed here are by no means comprehensive. Particular situations will have their own special values. There may also be many more general values which can be added to my list.

(British Airways lounge at Johannesburg airport, awaiting
QF 064 to Sydney)

Design is all about value creation. There are values which the design is supposed to deliver. Then there are values which make the design acceptable. At the same time there are values which determine whether the design is practical enough to use. Where it is a matter of changing from an existing way of doing things to a new way, there are transition values as well.

Looking for value is much more difficult than looking for faults and potential dangers. We are all very risk sensitive but much less value sensitive. We tend only to notice the obvious values. As I suggested earlier in this book, developing 'value sensitivity' is an important part of design thinking. The brain easily notices deviations from what is expected. The brain does not easily notice enhancements of what is expected.

Benefits (dev 1)

What are the benefits? For whom are the benefits? How are the benefits delivered? Under what circumstances are the benefits delivered?

The search for benefits is as wide-ranging as possible. One person's problem may be another person's benefit. If a soprano falls ill that is hardly a benefit to the soprano, the opera house or the impresario. But it may be a great benefit for the understudy. One factory's waste may be another factory's raw material. A delayed flight may allow a very late passenger to catch the flight. All benefits should be noted – not only the obvious ones for which the design was made. Occasionally by-product benefits may come to outweigh the core benefits. Sometimes the warm-up person is funnier than the comedian himself.

No benefit should be dismissed as minor or obscure. The harder you look for small benefits, the clearer the larger benefits become. One man decided not to report the theft of his credit cards because, he said, the thief was spending less than his wife would have done.

Benefits should be listed because they are all too easily forgotten.

Looking for benefits even in the most unlikely situation is a good habit of mind and trains value sensitivity.

Significant (dev 2)

Overall a design should deliver significant benefits – otherwise what is the purpose of the design.

A particular design may suggest only a small change. But the purpose of that small change is to get everyone used to the idea of change. That is a very significant benefit. The policy of zero tolerance in New York City seemed to target minor criminals – but there were two significant benefits. A signal was sent that any sort of crime was not to be tolerated. At the same time, youngsters who started off with minor crimes found themselves in trouble before the crime habit had become firmly established. These are significant benefits.

There are times when designers feel that they have to show 'a design input'. The designer has to leave his fingerprints all over the design. This is not a significant benefit unless the 'recognized' brand image of the design is of value to some people. There are people who like to carry bags with 'Moschino' written in large letters on the bag. That is a matter of choice. Chanel established a brand image in women's suits. There might even be disappointed readers who have purchased this book because they expect me to write sense.

In general, the prime and intended value delivered by a design should be significant. Lots of minor values rarely add up to a significant value.

Broad (dev 3)

(37,000 feet, QF 064, one hour out of Perth)

Pavements and sidewalks have been adjusted to allow people in wheelchairs to ride on or off. In the USA a part of the bus has to 'kneel down' to provide easier access. These are values for very specific groups. That is the purpose of the design. In general, however, the more broadly the value is delivered the higher the value.

If a design intended for general use actually benefits only a few people under very special circumstances, then that design does not have a high value. The more people who benefit the better. The benefits should flow under normal circumstances – unless the design is intended specifically for particular circumstances.

Key Values (dev 4)

This book is being written on a Psion Series 5 palmtop. The key value is the battery life. Ordinary torch batteries (AA) are used and they last very much longer than any laptop battery. Because I am writing at odd moments, in the air, waiting in lounges, on hilltops, etc., this battery factor is a 'key value'. A key value is one which overrides other values. The keyboard on a laptop would be larger and make typing easier, other functions might be better, but the battery life value overrides them all.

A key value is like a 'gateway' value. If you cannot get through a gateway, then it does not matter what wonderful things are inside. When employing someone, a key value might be honesty. In many situations a key value is cost.

Surprisingly, being able to write is no longer a key value for an author. Speech-recognition software makes it possible to write a book by speaking to a computer – though style might suffer.

Robust (dev 5)

A 'robust' value is one which is not fragile. A robust value holds up under a wide range of circumstances. A fragile value is one which depends on a very special set of circumstances.

A robust value is delivered even if the operation is not carried out with a great degree of skill. Taking a photograph requires much less skill than painting a portrait. An automatic camera requires less skill than a camera where every function needs to be set.

When the values of a design are robust, you can expect those values to be delivered whatever the circumstances. It is not easy to mess up robust values. In engineering terms there is a high degree of tolerance: the fit does not have to be exact.

A robust education programme, like the CoRT Thinking Lessons, will work even if the teacher is not exceptional and not highly trained. Programmes which require exceptional teachers or training are not very practical.

Time Value (dev 6)

How long will it take to effect the design and deliver the value? How long will the values last? Will a competitive response quickly erode the values? The time factor comes in at many points: time to carry through the design; time over which values are delivered. Most organizations, except the courts of law, realize that time itself is a high value and an expensive one. An inefficient planning authority which holds up development permits can cost the developer a great deal of money in interest payments.

What is the time factor of this design? Sometimes a design cannot get going unless something happens first. Waiting for that thing to happen introduces a great deal of uncertainty. Waiting for an old lady to die so that her heirs can sell you the house she refuses to leave can mean a long wait.

Novelty in a design can be a powerful factor but is not very durable. The faster a craze takes off, the faster it dies. This is because people who do not really appreciate the craze are sucked in – and they soon drop out, causing the craze to collapse.

Many things have no value until they are completed. So no value is derived during the long construction period. To avoid this, developers seek to sell off the plan.

Low Cost (dev 7)

Cost is always a major negative value in any design. Cost may or may not be a key value but it is always a key factor.

Low cost is almost always an attractive feature in any design. The trade-off between cost and quality is always there.

Many initial ideas need to be developed or modified in order to lower the cost. Many excellent designs are never implemented because the cost cannot be made acceptable.

Obviously there is a balance between cost and value delivered. A cheap design is not automatically the best one. The cheap design may require more maintenance or more servicing.

Any design where the cost has not been considered is an incomplete design.

Simplicity (dev 8)

(On board QF 064 during stopover in Perth en route to Sydney)

As life gets more complicated 'simplicity' is becoming a core value, not an add-on cosmetic value. Right from the beginning systems and methods need to be designed to be simple. Simplicity is not something that is added at the end.

It is amazing that in the computer world the tremendous advances in technology have in no way been matched by advances in simplicity of use. This is probably because simplicity is no one's business. Technology is someone's business, but simplicity is not.

The potential offered by technology cannot be fully enjoyed unless it comes without stress, anxiety and a great deal of learning. The experts will always manage no matter how complex the systems might be. The US Department of Justice trial of Microsoft contained a video clip of just how complex the systems could be even to an expert.

Any system that is going to be operated by ordinary people or that is going to affect ordinary people needs to be simple. There is no excuse for it to be otherwise. A complex system is likely to be a bad design.

If you understand a subject really well then you can explain the subject very simply. It is only if you do not understand the subject that you relish complexity and do not understand simplicity.

People (dev 9)

Designs are going to involve people. People have to construct and operate designs. People have to accept new designs. In the end, any design has to offer value to people.

So the people factor is very important. Even an abstruse mathematical theorem has to make sense to the small group of insiders who are expected to understand it.

Where there is any element of change then the new design has to be acceptable. Those expected to switch to the new design must see some benefits in the switch and must be shown that the switch is painless. Those people expected to operate the new system must find it easy to operate and must be trained.

Where the benefits are real but not obvious to those who receive them (a common situation), the benefits must be explained in a clear and credible manner. When hotels encourage guests to reuse towels in order to help save the environment, the guests may suspect the suggestion is only made to help hotel profits.

There are those who benefit from a new design. There are those who do not benefit – but may see others benefiting. There are those who may be disadvantaged by the change. There are those who will be against any change because that is their habit of mind, and that is how they can express themselves.

Problems in school textbooks do not involve anyone else. As soon as a youngster leaves school, however, he or she finds that real-life problems almost always involve other people. It is the same with design.

It is said that a camel is a horse designed by a committee. To what extent should a design be the work of a group or committee? This depends on the subject and individual methods of working. Group work has many advantages. If, however, style or really new ideas are required, then these come from individuals and are only diluted by a group.

Compatible (dev 10)

It is only rarely that a completely new system is put into place. Most often a new design has to be 'compatible' with what is already in place. The computer world found this out rather quickly. Few people were willing to scrap old systems and to start all over again with a new system.

This need for compatibility may restrict the innovation of a new design, but usually there is little choice. On motorways it would be much more logical for the fast lane to be on the outside – but such a change would not be compatible with current exiting systems and habits.

Habits and habits of perception are systems in a sense: a new design should also be compatible with these systems. Expectations are equally important: a new design must fit existing expectations or an effort must be made to change existing expectations.

Compatibility with existing personalities and cultures is also important. There are numerous stories of international advertising campaigns that were not at all compatible with local culture.

Authoritarian managers might not take easily to a design that encouraged participation.

In the end the key consideration is whether to adapt to what is there or to seek to change what is there. The important point is that this needs to be a conscious choice and a deliberate strategy. It is not much use assuming that a design is so wonderful that everyone will eagerly embrace it.

Small Changes (dev 11)

There is considerable skill in designing small changes that are easily taken up and implemented – almost without anyone noticing the change. This is a sort of 'design by stealth'.

The virtue of a design may be precisely that it is a small change, but the effect of that small change may be considerable. Big changes may be dramatic but not so easily accepted. Minimal changes can still be designed to be effective.

So the value delivered by a design may be 'significant', but the design itself might only require a small change.

The 'small change' value is worth seeking.

Negative Values (dev 12)

Pollution is a negative value of industrialization. The introduction of exotic diseases is a negative value of long-distance air travel. Noise is a negative value of airports.

Negative values are not planned – they just arise. A negative value of allowing a man into the kitchen is that there will be pots and pans all over the place – even if the meal is superb.

As I suggested in an earlier part of this book, negative values are not really faults. A fault prevents a design from working well. A negative value arises precisely because a design is working well. Road accidents happen because cars are able to travel fast. The Internet gets overloaded because it works so well.

Purists will not like the inherent contradiction in the term 'negative value' but pragmatists will see the practical necessity for it.

Actuality (dev 13)

Can this design 'actually' be put into effect? Can this design be implemented through existing channels and mechanisms?

There is a wide spectrum between fantasy designs which can never be implemented and something 'which could be done tomorrow'. The term 'actuality' indicates how far along that spectrum the idea is – in the direction of being do-able tomorrow.

An assessment of actuality means running the situation forward in your mind: can you see the design being put into action? Can you see universities running foundation courses in thinking? Can you see Australia appointing a king of its own?

Actuality is not the same as practicality. The term 'practicality' means that the idea can be carried out in a practical manner. There may be a design that is practical in itself but where the actuality is low. Mini tea bags are very practical but it is difficult to see the makers of tea bags making mini versions because it would cut their profits if people only used the amount of tea they really needed.

Widening the goalposts in soccer is simple and practical enough. It would give a more interesting high-scoring game with less tension and violence. But can you see any official soccer body putting this design into practice?

Do-Able (dev 14)

This is very closely related to practicality: 'this design can be put into effect'. Practicality and do-able do not say anything about the value of the design, nor even about the acceptability of the design. A design may indeed be do-able, but deliver little value, and so is not easily accepted.

Logically it could be argued that 'do-able' should also include 'acceptable'. If the design is not acceptable, then it cannot be done. While this is logical, there is a practical value in separating 'do-able', which refers to the design itself, and 'acceptable', which refers to a particular context. A design may be do-able in itself and acceptable in some countries but not in others. This could equally apply to some organizations and not to others. The separation of do-able from acceptable means that it becomes possible to focus on these values separately.

You can cook an excellent dish but not all diners would enjoy that dish. The dish is do-able but not universally acceptable.

Fit (dev 15)

This rather broad value overlaps a great deal with many of the other values listed here.

The difference between 'analysis' and practical operations is that analysis divides up into clearly separate elements which do not overlap. Practical operations often overlap. You can use a chisel as a screwdriver (not recommended but possible). You could use a credit card to slice a banana.

Does it fit the situation? Does it fit the needs?

So the value of 'fit' is a broad overview. Certain strategies and products might fit a small organization trying to get a foothold in the market, but would not fit an already established major player. The mini tea bag concept is one such example.

Fit particularly refers to resources. To implement the design may require money, time, management time and other resources. This may mean taking these away from other projects. Would there be the will to do this?

Fit also refers to culture and personalities. Does the design fit the local culture? Does the design fit the personalities involved? A flamboyant personality may welcome a large gesture which a quieter personality will reject.

Fit works at different levels. Will the proposed design be accepted? Can the proposed design be implemented? Will the implemented design deliver the promised values? Many of these points are relative. The same design may fit one situation but not another.

Is 'fit' a judgement or part of the design process? It has to be both. At an early stage there needs to be an effort to design to fit the specific situation. At a later stage, when the design is shaping up, the same question needs to be asked repeatedly: does this fit, does this still fit?

Modifications may need to be made to get a better fit. Sometimes the fit gets so bad that a completely new approach has to be tried.

The difficulty is that if the design is simply crafted to 'fit' as the major value – then that design may deliver no other values. So it is essential to keep the key values in mind all the time – and still seek to make the design fit.

In a way it is a matter of 'fitting the brief' but also of 'fitting the circumstances that set the brief'.

In the end any design should deliver value and fit.

Responsibility (dev 16)

Who is going to be responsible for implementing the design? This consideration is part of the design process. There is no point in cooking a wonderful meal if there are no plates on which to serve the food.

So the design needs to have built into it designated responsibilities. To have these made clear is a value. Design is not at all like throwing food to a hungry dog. There is no automatic eager acceptance. Change is rarely seen as a joy.

Implementation (dev 17)

It is easy and comfortable to treat the design as an end in itself. The dress designer does not have to indicate when and how the dress will eventually be worn.

It is, however, an added value in a design if consideration has been given to steps and stages of implementation.

In giving seminars on 'thinking skills' it always seemed obvious to me that such skills could be used broadly in most situations. It turned out that people were much more inclined to use the skills if practical suggestions on implementation were also given.

If you sell a picture you may also want to give advice on where and how the picture might be hung.

The suggested implementation may never be used. The

accepting organization may have their own, and better, ways of implementing the design. After all, the organization probably knows its people, its culture and its methods better than the designer. Nevertheless, practical suggestions on implementation are a design value.

Motivation (dev 18)

What is the motivation around the design? Who is eager to have and to use the design?

This is more than acceptability (dev 9), compatibility (dev 10) and fit (dev 15). All those are 'passive' processes. Motivation is active, and implies energy and the will to action.

The design needs to incorporate features that will stimulate motivation. The design needs to build on existing motivations. The design needs to find ways of sustaining motivation. Between accepting a design and watching it in use, there may be a lot of hard work. Motivation ensures that the hard work is done. So 'motivation points' may need to be built into the design.

Motivation is needed not only for those leading the implementation process but for everyone involved. How do they get a sense of success and achievement. Builders watch a building going up. The achievement is tangible and they can imagine the completed structure. The people who built the great cathedrals were motivated by their service to God but also by their sense of achievement.

Look Good (dev 19)

Politicians like to look good. Chief executives like to look good. It is an added value in a design if consideration is given to how certain people can be made to 'look good'. This may seem to be pandering to human vanity – and it is. But human vanity and human motivation and human behaviour are rather closely linked.

Designers want to 'look good'; why should other people not also be given the chance to look good?

Criticism (dev 20)

Anything worthwhile will attract criticism. The more worthwhile the greater the criticism. People who do not have a creative or constructive talent have to exert their egos in criticism.

Criticism is remarkably easy, so an abundance of it can be expected.

Part of the value of a design is to foresee criticism and to be prepared to meet it. It may also be useful, in advance, to secure the opinions and endorsements of those who do know something about the subject – in order to balance the noise of those who know nothing about the subject (empty vessels, etc.).

Some points of criticism may well be valid. There may be genuine environmental concerns. Homework needs to be done on these issues and it is best if they are met head on.

It is usually easy to distinguish between genuine criticism and the more usual ego noises. Just count the adjectives.

I want to make it clear that the above list of possible design values is not comprehensive. The list lays out suggestions and considerations. It is obvious that the design process is very different indeed from the judgement process and simple logical procedures. That was the purpose behind the list.

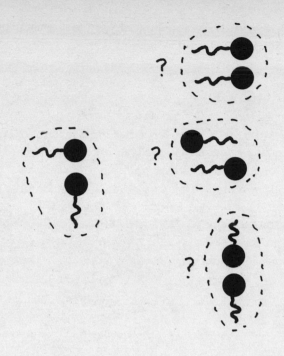

Comparison

Judgement is comparison with what we know. The comparison of something new with our 'stock' of experiences. The tole position on the left is compared with the known tole positions on the right. There is no exact match, so we interpret it as best we can.

Replacement Design

There are many different approaches to design and I do not claim to be comprehensive in the suggestions listed here.

There is a difference between 'replacement design' and 'new design'. With a replacement design there is already something in existence.

The standard approach would be that of 'modification'. This means correcting the faults, overcoming the defects and weaknesses. This is a variation on problem-solving and is a useful approach. At the same time there may be an effort to strengthen and enhance the strong points or values. This may involve simplification. This may involve extending the benefits to more people. In a competitive environment it may mean making the idea more difficult to imitate.

Design modification can take place a very small step at a time as in the Japanese *kaisen* (small-step improvement). The steps can be rather bigger.

Occasionally the modification approach results in a complete change of concept, but this would be rare.

Another approach is to start from the beginning: to design from scratch. This means setting aside the existing approach and setting out to deliver more or less the same values.

In this situation, instead of starting with a core value, as would be the case with a new design, it is often best to start out with a whole collection of values. These would include the new values that the existing designs did not provide.

For example, in seeking to design a new car the starting-point might include the following: high resale value; easy to park; cheap to service and repair; flexible in use; able to reflect personality of owner. When we look at these 'design objectives', almost at once a concept emerges. This is a modular concept. The modular concept would allow for a higher resale value because parts that were heavily worn could be replaced. The modular concept would allow for flexibility of use: family, goods, single-person use, etc. The modular concept might provide for 'personalization' with decorative panels that could be attached. The modular concept might even help with parking, with a stripped-down shopping version that the owner could assemble when shopping was the objective.

If you were to design a new toothbrush you might start off with: some way of indicating that the right pressure was used; ensuring that enough time was spent brushing; multi-purpose; easy grip; easy to pack. From this assortment might come the idea of a detachable head and an electronic body. There would be both an electronic timer (set for three minutes or choice) and a pressure indicator. The handle would be made of a plastic which could be softened so that it adapted to the grip and then hardened for permanence. Another version might separate the brush from the indicator aspects with a 'blue tooth' radio link.

In replacement design, if you start with the existing design it is difficult to break away from the existing concepts. Should cars have wheels? Should toothbrushes have bristles? At some point there needs to be a background decision: how radical is the replacement going to be?

The replacement design of a school might look nothing like an existing school. Technology today (where it can be afforded) might suggest a lot of individual learning stations for individuals or small groups. The teacher would be both a 'caretaker' of the learning process and a source of guidance. So there might be a big hall for everyone to come together and then lots of cubicles. The starting values might have been: technology; flexibility of choice; different tracks; decoupling from the teacher; pursuit of interests, etc.

The design of a modern restaurant might start with a consideration of modern eating habits: diets; weight concerns; range of food experiences; cost consciousness. The final result might be a restaurant which only served 'starters'. Depending on your appetite (and budget) you could choose one, two, three or more. There would be a wide variety. Since many of these would be cold there would be less wastage. Some starters could be standardized and supplied by a branded outside supplier (so giving predictability). In other words the notion of a three-course meal with a main dish would have been designed away.

Do all the desired values have to be pursued in parallel all the time? Probably not. Sometimes values coalesce into a design concept – as with the modular car. At other times one or two values are pursued and then the others added later – as with the toothbrush concept.

Any existing design has reached a state of equilibrium. Any movement away from that stable design is likely to suggest disadvantages. That is why it may be better to start from scratch with a number of desired values. These values could be entirely new values or they could be partly derived from the values offered by the existing design. Being different for the sake of being different produces neither creativity nor good design. Printing a newspaper diagonally may be novel and 'different' but it does not seem to offer any new value.

In this design approach it is important to be honest. It is not much use thinking of a 'design', then describing the characteristics of that new design and finally arriving back at the design you first thought of. The desired values should be genuinely laid out – without any preconceived thoughts as to how the values might come together as a design. Then from this 'honest' beginning the design can start to emerge.

If you just want to add one 'missing' value, the modification approach is more suitable. For example, if you wanted to design a plate you might be satisfied with almost anything, but you may want to add a small ridge at some point so that food may be more easily scooped up against this ridge, instead of chasing peas around the plate. Or you may want to have some way of personalizing the plate. So you make the rim white and wide and write on it with water-soluble ink. A small ridge could protect this area from slopping food. You could then write names, messages, quotes, etc.

If you were to start designing a plate from scratch you might consider: novel shape; very easy to wash; adaptable to different uses. The result might be a base frame or holder: disposable plates would be placed over this holder. The shape of these disposable plates could vary according to the food needs: soup, rice, meat, etc. This separation of surface from structure is very different from the modifications mentioned above.

If you were designing a new democratic system you might want to allow for the voters to have a continuing influence – not just at election time. The result might be that the salaries of Members of Parliament would vary with current approval rating – from some baseline. So if the baseline was 70 per cent approval then a 35 per cent approval would mean half salary. Another concept would be to have a third party with seats but no actual members. These votes would be decided by public opinion poll on any new issue. In this way the opposition could introduce legislation and get it through if their idea had enough support. Because these are single-point changes they lie halfway between modification and assembly strategies. Because the change necessary to achieve the desired value is large, tinkering with the existing system is unlikely to deliver that value. In such cases, 'the assembly approach' means: existing values plus this new value. That is often different from modifying the existing system to include the new value. In practice the distinction is sharp even if it is blurred philosophically.

Pure Examples

A funnel collects things into the centre. The toles are shown
swimming towards the centre. When we think of things we think of
the 'central' or 'pure' example or 'stereotype'. That is how judgement
works.

New Design

With replacement design there is already a design in place. An effort is needed to avoid being trapped by the existing approach – that is the reason behind the assembly approach. With a new design there is no design in place so there are no such concerns.

With a new design it is best to start with one core or 'driving' value. This provides energy and momentum. Once the design has started its life other values can be brought in at an early or late stage.

Supposing that we wanted to design 'a signal that people could use to indicate to others their sociability at that moment'. The driving value might be a signal that was visible and unambiguous. Later on the values of 'elegant', 'unobtrusive' and even 'fashionable', might be brought in.

So the idea might emerge of different coloured hats depending on the social needs. There might be a hat for 'fancy free but looking to meet new people'; there might be a hat for 'in a relationship but open to new friends'; there might be a hat for 'very bored and looking for adventure'; there might be a hat for 'seriously looking for a life partner'.

This design might work but might be too visible. In any case it would be a bother to carry several hats in case of a change of mood (possibly not such a bother because the status would hardly change so often). The 'too visible' stridency would be a problem, since it would be so blatant.

A more subdued approach might be the four-sided biretta with a tassel in the middle described in Chapter 16. The Japanese radio-linked, match-seeking portable computer may be more exact – but much less fun (used in a nightclub).

Time goes too fast when you are having fun. Perhaps we could set out to design 'boring holidays' (Chapter 10). A week would seem like a month. Short breaks would seem long. Predictability and lack of change would be the driving values here. Of course, it is not as simple as that, because acute boredom is rather stressful.

How could we design a 'test' that allowed youngsters to show their best qualities whatever these might be? Current exams test those who are good at the academic game. Projects test those who have initiative. Teacher assessments are highly subjective. Peer-group assessments are 'popularity' biased. Self-assessment has the difficulty that many youngsters do not even know their best points.

In this design task the driving value might be 'reactive flexibility'. Ideally, it would be best to put youngsters in a variety of situations and then to see how each person reacted. This approach is usually not very practical. A less satisfactory alternative would be to create a series of stories involving young people. Each story would stop at a certain point and youngsters would be asked: 'Which character do you identify with, and what would you do next?' Instead of stories there might be video clips. An explanation of the chosen action might also be requested. The stories would need to be crafted so that an obvious 'goody-goody' answer was not possible. The reader could also be asked to 'assess' the good points of the actors in the story.

How pure does a driving value have to be? Does 'visible but practical' constitute one value or two? Qualifiers do not really count as two values. If we needed a material that was 'strong but cheap' that is not really two values from a design point of view. It would not be much use thinking of a strong material, like titanium, and then going on to say that it must also be cheap. Qualified values are really composite values and can be treated as single values. As in so many other cases the philosophical distinction between a qualified value and an assembly of values is not easy. In practice, the distinction is much easier.

A 'low skill, small people-transporter' is a qualified value that can be treated as the driving value. This might lead to the idea of a sort of airport luggage trolley, where the luggage was replaced by an engine and the driver stood on a little platform at the back. This would require far less skill than a bicycle or motor cycle.

Other values can also be added. The value of weather protection can be added to the people-transporter. The engine can be fuel efficient and economical. Perhaps the engine could be electric with replaceable batteries shunted on or off as with a fork-lift truck.

If an electric vehicle was designed as a 'new design' rather than a 'replacement design', then the matter of battery recharging would be driving value. Perhaps the batteries could be towed behind on an easily changeable trailer. Comfort and car behaviour could then be added to the design. That is different from designing a car and then adding batteries – the usual approach.

Once there is the 'driving value' then we look around for a way of delivering that value. There may be traditional ways which can be borrowed. There may be a need to design a way of delivering the value. There may be standard elements which can easily be put together to deliver the value. As in all design work there is an emphasis on alternatives. With problem-solving we are grateful to get the first possible solution. With design the first possibility is only one of many and the many have to be explored and laid out.

If 'flash steam' had been invented six months earlier we might today all be driving around in steam cars – which had several advantages. Design usually means going forward but we could also step backwards and might want our people-transporter driven by a flash-steam engine.

I was once asked by a government agency for a 'source of new ideas'. I suggested a look in the bankruptcy files. In these files there might be ideas which were before their time. There might be ideas which could be supported by today's technology but not by the technology of the earlier time. There might be good ideas which were badly managed or undercapitalized. The commercial failure of an idea does not always mean it was a bad idea.

A design only works if it delivers value. We are not so good at clarifying and laying out value. With transport we might think of: speed, safety, comfort, multi-point access and predictability. Cost is then added as a major constraint. The Concorde supersonic plane provided marvellous speed but the need to have refuelling stops made it unsuitable on those very routes where speed would have had a high value – like London to Sydney. Efficient and safe mid-air refuelling might have made a difference, especially as about 20 per cent of the fuel is consumed just in taking off. If 'range' had been added to the design values then the Concorde might never have been made; given these considerations, the political 'prestige value' of the Concorde at the time would have been neglected – but that is not a transport value.

Designers of cars think of all the important values but rarely think of the matter of getting in and out of a car. Cost, appearance, aerodynamic considerations, safety engineering, etc., determine the shape of a car and the opening of the doors. It is difficult for older people to get out of the front seat of a car. There should be a swivel on the seat. This can be improvised by sitting on a magazine, the pages of which then allow a swivelling effect. The design of easy getting in and out is a real value.

Technology as such quickly switches from being a value to becoming an 'expectation'. Power steering is a value but it becomes an expectation. A device which would reduce the risk of a driver falling asleep would be a real value, as more car accidents are caused by drivers falling asleep than by alcohol. Many years ago I did suggest just such a device to a maker of car equipment. The normal small oscillations of the steering-wheel would be recorded; when these altered or ceased a loud alarm would sound and wake the driver up. The technology for such a device is easy and available. Values are not always obvious. Obvious values are not the only ones.

Supermarkets do not like to label food positions too clearly since 'impulse buys' are said to account for 80 per cent of purchases. As you look for what you really want you are tempted to buy other things. This not only gives the supermarket increased sales – it also expands your range of experience. If, however, you just want some basic items, like razor-blades, it is a bother to have to traverse the whole supermarket to find them. So there could be a special section near the door called 'routine purchase items'. Research would show which items to stock in this place. If supermarkets also visibly displayed 'traffic density' times, then people could choose to shop to avoid such times. Defining values is a skill in itself.

Asking people their needs and what they want is not a complete way of defining values. People can only comment on what they know and have experienced. They may well point out problems and defects, but are much less able to suggest new values, which do not yet exist. In one case research showed that consumers were not interested in a plastic spout placed on a carton of orange juice. When this suggestion was actually put into effect the sales increased dramatically.

With our usual habits of analysis and judgement in the search for the truth, we believe that values are there 'to be discovered'. This is only partly true. Values also need inventing and designing. Before you pick up the phone would you not like to know whether it is a friendly call or a business call. That could so easily be designed.

What about an egg-timer device which lifted an egg out of the boiling water at a pre-set time? This is a trivial idea, for the same result could be achieved in many ways. But all these other ways require attention. Perhaps the 'absence of a need for attention' is the driving value.

When a piece of equipment requires attention a light blinks or an alarm sounds. Lights cannot be seen around corners and alarm sounds are too scary. What about a device that gives off a smell if a copier or other machinery requires attention? Smells go around corners and bad smells demand attention. There is also the 'peer pressure' on anyone who allows the bad smell to be emitted.

When is a design trivial and when is a design non-trivial?

Examine for the value that is intended. Examine for success in delivering that value. If the value is real and delivered effectively, the design is not trivial.

Design Notation 1

In pidgin English in Papua New Guinea there is a very powerful word 'bilong'. This sounds like 'belong' but has come to have a very wide meaning. There is the possession aspect as in: 'This child him bilong that father.' There is the association aspect: 'Johnny him bilong big ship.' The general meaning is that something belongs to, or is part of, an association frame. An association frame is very much broader than a concept. A concept is a defined collection of functions or items. An association frame means those things happen to be together, in general, often or right now. An association frame is nothing to do with definitions, boxes or categories as in our traditional thinking. If you make a picture of a school and show a teacher, you could say that a teacher is part of the concept of a school. So are pupils. But a particular pupil named Henry might be in your picture. So might a dog called Snappy. They are not part of the concept of a school but they 'bilong' in that picture or that association frame.

The word 'bilong' is powerful precisely because it is not precise. It is vague and general and blurry and all-encompassing. This gives it a huge information value. Precision is only a value in information in certain circumstances (for action but not for creativity).

So the first step in the notation is that the 'association frame' is represented by a circle. This circle can be given a number which refers to a meaning in the list of numbers. This number listing avoids the problem of writing small all over the diagram.

Anything within this association frame is shown as a small circle within the larger circle. This simply means that this thing may be found (not always and not essentially) within that association frame. The thing so depicted is not part of a definition but just happens to be in that association frame at this moment (in your mind).

Now we come to the key 'convenience' part of the notation. A line joining any circle to another circle means that the two are the same: not equal but exactly the same. In other words the line allows us to transfer or translocate any item to another position. So a small circle can be transferred to become a big circle somewhere else and can now include other small circles.

So the notation includes two items only:

1. Inclusion in an association frame (on whatever basis).

2. Translocation of any item to any new position.

Suppose that we were redesigning a coffee mug (as a replacement design). The values that we start off with might be:

- Very stable
- Able to tell temperature
- No spoon needed
- No saucer needed
- Variable sugar supplied

The listed numbers might now go as follows:

1 . . . the large circle represents the 'design brief'
2 . . . the need for stability
3 . . . some way of showing the heat of the liquid inside
4 . . . no need for a spoon
5 . . . no need for a saucer
6 . . . variable amount of sugar

The small circle (2), which represents 'stable' is now translocated to a bigger circle. Within this association frame emerge two ideas. The mug might have three knobs on the bottom to give it 'tripod' stability on an uneven surface (7). Another idea is to attach the mug to a wider base, perhaps like a fixed saucer (8).

The small circle (3) which represents 'heat detection' is also translocated to an association frame. From this come three ideas. The first (9) is to have a strip of heat-sensitive paint on the outside of the mug to indicate the heat. A parallel idea (10) is to have the inside of the mug painted with heat-sensitive paint. This idea in turn provides an association frame which delivers the idea (17) of a spoon painted with heat-sensitive paint. This last idea is not part of the brief of redesigning the mug, but is worthy of note. Another idea included in the association frame (3) is that of building into the mug some simple thermometer (11).

The 'no spoon need' (4) also becomes an association frame which delivers two ideas. The first (12) is to have a vertical ridge inside the mug so that gently oscillating the mug will stir the contents. This idea itself provides an association from which comes another idea (13) – the mug is square or elliptical so oscillating this would also mix the contents.

The 'no saucer' (5) value is a minor one as mugs do not have saucers anyway. One idea coming from this association frame is to have a small protruding platform which might hold sugar, a biscuit, etc. (15). Another idea from the same association frame might have a detachable shelf which could be hung on the edge of the mug (16).

The 'variable sugar' value (6) might lead to the idea of a side compartment which would be filled with sugar. Tilting the mug would bring the contents into contact with the sugar for however long you wanted (18). Cleaning such a mug would be a problem.

Various of these ideas could be combined: tripod base; elliptical shape; heat-sensitive paint; and protruding platform. The result could then be made more aesthetically pleasing, easy to produce and easy to clean. These would be final added values – but still

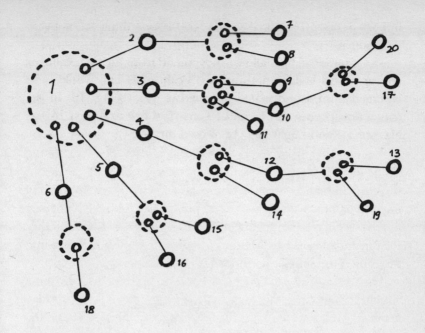

1. new coffee cup
2. stable
3. show temperature
4. no need for a spoon
5. no saucer

6. variable sugar
7. tripod knobs on base
8. attached saucer
9. heat-sensitive paint outside
10. heat-sensitive paint inside

11. thermometer

12. internal vertical ridge
13. square or elliptical
cross-section
14. oscillate
15. protruding platform

16. hang-on platform
17. painted heat-sensitive spoon
18. sugar compartment
19. clip-on ridge
20. clip-on strip with
heat-sensitive paint

important ones. The costs would rocket if something was not easy to produce.

The notation simply allows 'movement' from an idea, value or concept. This is flow, not analysis. With analysis it would have emerged from 4 and would have led to 12, 13 and 19. In the actual flow process 12, 13 and 19 emerged first and then 14 was extracted – and might have been used further.

Design Notation 2

When writing music the 'position' of a mark indicates the note that is intended. In a parallel-design notation the position of a mark also indicates the nature of the item.

There are five parallel bands. Each band represents a type of idea. An arrow indicates progression from one thought to another.

The topmost band indicates very broad concepts, approaches or directions. These 'directions' are similar to the directions in the 'concept fan' of lateral thinking. If you are driving you will be heading in a general direction: north, east, etc.

The next band down represents the 'concept'. In the driving analogy the concepts are the 'roads'. These are the ways and means of heading in the general direction. There may be several different roads all of which are heading north. In the same way there may be several different concepts which allow us to move in the broad direction. All these concepts carry out the 'approach'.

The middle or third layer represents actual ideas. You cannot use a concept as such. You can only use ideas. If you stand on a road and say that you are travelling north you will not get any-where. There has to be specific action: walk, ride a bicycle, drive a car, hitch a lift, etc. The idea is a way of putting a concept into action. There may be many ways of putting a concept into action.

The fourth layer is the 'mechanism'. This means an actual existing mechanism for carrying out the idea. Sometimes the idea and the mechanism may be the same. 'Drive a car' is an idea. 'Drive my uncle's car' is a mechanism.

The final layer is the 'value'. The purpose of any design is to deliver value. The last layer includes the starting value that you wish to achieve. It also includes the final delivered values. At any point along the way the values involved may also be noted.

Suppose the design task is to 'encourage small business'. This is a goal in many economies since big business and government are not going to provide many new jobs and employment is seen as coming from small businesses.

The value to be obtained by the design is 'the encouragement of small business' (1) so this is placed in the value band.

There are at least three approaches to the design task. We could reduce the hassle of setting up a small business (4). We could increase the rewards (3). We could reduce the risk (2). It would be possible to work with all the approaches on the same diagram but this would get crowded and confusing. So we construct a fresh diagram for each broad concept.

So we work with 'lowering the risk' (2). An immediate idea is 'guaranteed financing' (5), which means that somebody guarantees loans and the entrepreneur does not have to put up his or her house as collateral for a loan. This leads to the concept of 'low-risk finance': that is to say low risk for the entrepreneur (6). If the entrepreneur fails, the loans do not have to be repaid. From this concept come several ideas. There might be special 'angel bonds' which investors could buy and which would be tax deductible (7). The mechanism (8) would be that investors would deduct the cost of the angel bonds from their taxable income. Two values might arise from this: an incentive to invest in small business (15); and bypassing government structures (16). Another idea arising from the concept is 'junk bonds' (19). The return to investors is high, but the risk is also high as the business might go bankrupt. A further idea is 'compulsory investment' (9). The mechanism would be that of 'investment quotas' (10). In order to receive some classification benefits, investment institutions would have to put a

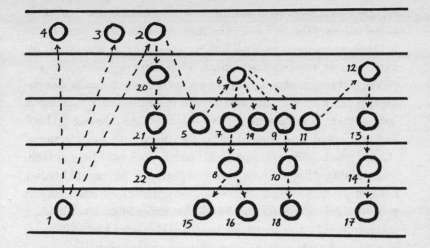

1. encourage small business
2. lower risk
3. increase rewards
4. reduce hassle
5. guaranteed finance

6. low-risk finance
7. angel bonds
8. tax-free investment
9. compulsory investment
10. quotas

11. government development funds

12. government involvement
13. government holding company
14. regional holding companies
15. incentives to invest

16. bypass government
17. employment created
18. social commitment
19. junk bonds
20. minimizing loss

21. sale
22. tax credits

certain quota of investments into a small-business portfolio. One of the values of this (18) would be that major investors would have to take some interest in small businesses – which is usually not the case. Special 'small-business funds' might emerge.

We can now proceed to the concept of 'low-risk funds' (for the user) at point (6). Another idea arising from this concept is that of 'government development funds' (11). From this idea we go back to a concept of 'government getting involved with small business' (12). From this new concept we consider ideas as to how government could get involved. One idea might be a government holding company which owned shares in many small businesses (13). A possible mechanism for this would be regional or local holding companies (14). A value arising from this idea would be an increase in employment in regions where this was important (17).

When the diagram has developed it is always possible to go back and add new ideas and concepts. For example we could go back to the broad concept of 'lowering the risk' (2) and move to a new concept of 'minimizing losses' (20). From this comes the idea (21) of being able to sell losses to someone else. The mechanism for doing this would be that any other business (even in non-related fields) could buy the losses, at a discount, and set them against its own taxes (22).

The value of the notation is that all the points are laid out and can be worked on, elaborated and taken further at any time. At any point 'sub-design tasks' might emerge and might merit a whole new charge for themselves.

The flow of thought is in any direction: from concept to value; from idea to concept; from concept to approach; up and down across the layers.

At any moment the mind is encouraged to find ways of carrying out a concept. The mind is also encouraged to seek out the concept behind an idea. All the time there is consideration of delivered value. The mechanism layer keeps the emphasis on practicality. Just as in a xylophone you move between the notes, so your mind moves across the layers. What is the value here? What is the concept here? How can that value be delivered? How can that concept be implemented?

Without notations our mind can only follow one sequence of thought at a time. Notations allow us an overview. Notations provide prompts. Notations allow us to shift attention.

Overview

In this book the emphasis has been on thinking that is concerned with 'what can be' rather than 'what is'. Traditional thinking is largely based on judgement. Traditional thinking is concerned with recognizing standard situations and applying standard solutions. This system is highly effective and very powerful. The bulk of our thinking should continue in that mode. In a changing world, with increasing opportunities (technology) and increasing pressures, there is also a need for the 'what-can-be' type of thinking. This is thinking that is creative and constructive. This is thinking that does not merely seek to identify 'what is' but also to bring about new things that have not yet existed. Throughout the book I have used the term 'design' to cover the thinking that brings about new thinking. Design thinking is the thinking that puts things together to deliver a value.

As we enter the new millennium there is every reason to put emphasis on design thinking. That is the thinking that will allow us to get the most out of what change and technology have to offer.

There are different levels of involvement in this other sort of thinking.

1. An awareness that for all its excellence, our traditional thinking (analysis, judgement, argument, truth, etc.) is not sufficient. The front left wheel of a motor car is excellent but insufficient by itself.

2. A willingness to give time, attention and effort to this 'design' aspect of thinking: a motivation to do so. This means recognizing

the validity, nature, importance and difference of design thinking. It is not a matter of seeking desperately to enlarge the scope of traditional thinking and to claim that it is all-sufficient. No matter how skilled this attempt might be, it is a futile effort. The accelerator in a car will always be different from the brake. Critical and judgement thinking cannot have the creative energy of design thinking. This change in attitude should mean huge changes in education at every level – but it is difficult to see by whom such needed changes would be led.

3. A general motivation on all occasions to try thinking that is constructive and creative. This means a win/win attitude in disputes. This means a willingness to seek to 'design a way forward' in difficult situations. Problem-solving will always benefit from the traditional approach of finding and removing the cause of the problem. Where this is not possible there will be an effort to design a way forward – leaving the cause in place.

The constructive attitude includes a willingness to examine and to help develop new ideas. Possibilities should be generated and explored. There is a need to 'create value', not just seek to find value.

4. We can then go beyond the general attitude and motivation of design and constructive thinking to learn some of the habits, methods and techniques of this sort of thinking. Goodwill is not quite enough: skill is even better. Many of the processes of constructive and design thinking are totally different from our traditional thinking habits. For example, the parallel thinking of the Six Hats method is very different from classic argument. The process of 'provocation and movement' is very different from classic judgement. The flow logic of creative thinking is very different from the identity logic of deduction.

The purpose of traditional thinking is to deliver 'truth'. The purpose of design thinking is to deliver value. Both are needed.

All these processes can be learned and practised in a deliberate manner. Creative and design thinking is not some mystical gift which only a few talented people possess. Everyone can learn and use the skills of creative thinking. Some people will indeed be better at this skill, just as some people are better than others at any skill.

5. Some of the approaches to design thinking are given in this book. There are other frameworks and techniques which have now been in use successfully over many years. These are summarized in the Appendix.

6. After 2,400 years of immense complacency and self-satisfaction with our traditional thinking methods it is time to appreciate that they are not sufficient.

(QF 1 at 39,000 feet, flying from Sydney to Bangkok and then on to London, just before dinner is served)

Conclusion

If in this book I have given the impression that our existing thinking methods and habits are poor, then I have not done what I set out to do. Our existing thinking software is based on 'what is'. There is the search for the truth. There is the need to identify standard situations so that we can apply practical standard remedies. There is judgement related to principles. There is discrimination. There is argument to determine who has the 'truth'. There is 'right' and 'wrong'. Something is in this 'box' or not in this 'box'.

On the whole this system has served us well – because it is so very practical. It is true that the system encourages prejudice, discrimination, stereotypes, persecutions and wars. Appalling as these things are, they are not my main quarrel with the thinking system that has dominated the last millennium.

My point is that the system is excellent but inadequate. Our excellence in working with 'what is' has meant that insufficient attention has been paid to the 'what-can-be' side of thinking.

The front left wheel of a motor car is excellent and I would not criticize its excellence. But I would point out the inadequacy of just having a front left wheel on a motor car.

The 'what-can-be' aspect of thinking is concerned with design rather than analysis; with value rather than truth.

You can analyse the past but you have to design the future.

Without design and creativity we cannot take advantage of what is offered by science and technology. We seek to solve problems by attacking and removing what is 'bad'. Crude and primitive as this approach may be, it does often work. But when it does not work we are paralysed. Most of the major problems in the world will not be solved by yet more analysis. There is a need to 'design' the way forward. Unfortunately our traditional habits of thinking and our traditional education system do not equip us for design thinking. While the human brain itself is very good at judgement, recognition and fine discrimination, it is not good at design.

For far too long we have believed that creativity is some magic talent which would never be understood. This is dogmatic ignorance. There is no mystery about the design of ideas, concepts and perceptions. Once we understand the brain as a self-organizing information system then we can understand creativity as 'lateral movement' across asymmetric patterns. It is the same process as humour.

For over thirty years I have worked towards the improvement of human thinking. I have worked with senior executives in many of the world's largest corporations. I have worked with four-year-olds in school. I once worked with a group made up entirely of Nobel prize laureates. Others (such as Susan Mackie) have used my work with illiterate miners in South Africa and with Down's syndrome youngsters.

There is no mystery about teaching thinking. It can be done practically and simply. The effects are very powerful. The parallel thinking of the Six Hats frame leads to thinking that is very much quicker and more constructive. Those that have used the method come to see argument as crude, aggressive and inefficient. The learnable skill of lateral thinking includes techniques that can be used formally and deliberately. For example, there is 'provocation'. We now know that provocation is mathematically necessary in any self-organizing system like the human brain. The 'attention-directing tools' of the CoRT programme (now widely used in schools) have an immediate and practical effect on the thinking of youngsters and adults. They can now take charge of their own lives.

Our traditional approach to thinking has been extraordinarily limited. We have focused almost entirely on 'logic' when as much as 90 per cent of the mistakes of thinking are mistakes of perception. The CoRT programme addresses this deficiency.

It is truly astonishing that 'thinking', the most important human skill of all, is not the central subject in all schools. Usually it is not there at all!

Is this because thinking is not considered important?

Is this because many people believe that thinking cannot be taught?

Is this because we believe we are already teaching thinking?

Each of these three attitudes is seriously out of date. Thinking is very important. Thinking can be taught. The thinking we now teach is limited and insufficient.

As I have suggested in the body of the book I believe all education systems are a disgrace. This is not the fault of those involved, who are talented, motivated and well-intentioned. But they are locked into a system which has evolved to a state where further evolution is not possible. As a result a huge amount of the talent which should be available to society is simply wasted.

We believe that intelligence is enough. It is not. Intelligence applied to playing the wrong game does not produce useful results.

Because historically we never had enough information, we have come to believe that more and more information via computers, Internet, etc., will provide all the answers. Information can indeed provide standard solutions. Information can provide the ingredients for design, but information is not design. What will matter is how we create value from information.

Einstein was right in saying that everything had changed except our way of thinking. We have been too smug, too self-satisfied and too complacent about our thinking habits. We have a system that is very much better at defending itself than at designing a better system.

It is not too late to develop thinking habits that are more constructive. It is not too late to encourage the creation of value. It is not too late to design a much better way forward. Even at the end of the twentieth century much of our thinking and behaviour is unbelievably crude, simplistic and primitive. Surely we can do better?

But to do better you have to want to do better. The new millennium needs people who want to do better. Thinking has been and will continue to be the key tool for designing a better future. Thinking can be improved and made more constructive. It can be done. But only if we start to do it. A few people have started.

Appendix

The following brief notes indicate some of the programmes that have been in use to help with constructive, creative and design thinking.

1. CoRT Thinking Lessons

CoRT stands for Cognitive Research Trust. The programme was designed for schools and is now widely in use throughout the world: Australia, New Zealand, Japan, Malaysia, Singapore, South Africa, Italy, UK, Ireland, Canada, USA, Venezuela, Philippines, etc. In most cases the use is patchy, with certain schools only implementing the programme. In other cases it is used across a whole district. In one country it is mandatory. Research has been done by Professor Michele de Bene at the University of Verona and Professor John Edwards at James Cook University, Australia.

There is a specific conference room on my web site for teachers to discuss their experiences (www.edwdebono.com/).

The majority of mistakes in ordinary thinking (outside technical matters) are mistakes in perception. Our traditional emphasis on logic does little for perception. If the perception is inadequate no amount of excellence in logic will make up for that deficiency.

Perception is a matter of directing attention. If you are not looking in the right direction it does not matter how clever you are, you will not see what you need to see.

The terms 'right' and 'left' are spatial directions. North, south, east and west are also spatial directions. You can ask someone to 'look left' or to 'look south'. That instruction indicates a 'direction'. You look in that direction and see what you see.

The CoRT programme is divided into six parts of ten lessons each. The first part deals with 'broadening' perception. The fourth part introduces specific creative processes.

In the first part the 'attention-directing tools' include: PMI, for a systematic scan of the Plus points, the Minus points and the Interesting points; OPV, for attention to Other People's Views; C&S for a deliberate focus on the consequences and sequel of a choice or action. The acronyms are necessary in order for the 'instruction' to exist in the mind as an 'operating concept'. Mere attitudes have no identity. These very simple tools are very powerful in their effect and can totally change initial judgements and perceptions.

The programme has been in use since 1972 with different cultures, ages and abilities. It has been used in Gifted Education programmes and also with Down's syndrome children (by Susan Mackie). I myself have taught some of the tools to 5,300 children from all sorts of schools, one morning in a sports stadium in Johannesburg.

David Perkins, professor of education at Harvard University has this to say about the CoRT programme in his book *Outsmarting the IQ* (NY, Free Press, 1995):

'In designing for the practical teaching of thinking Edward de Bono repeatedly emphasizes the importance of robust material that can be put into place easily. This is certainly one of the features of the CoRT programme.'

'CoRT fairly transparently addresses the thinking defaults identified in the previous chapter: hasty, narrow, fuzzy and sprawling thinking.'

'The four intelligence traps are vast; they make room for all kinds of mishaps and a diversity of sorts of thinking. None the less, CoRT plainly touches on all four.'

282

'Intelligence can be taught by CoRT.'

These comments are particularly relevant since it was Professor Perkins's work which showed the huge importance of perception in thinking.

For information contact **UK**: fax 0171 602 1779; **USA**: fax (515) 278 2245.

(Note: some of the CoRT tools are to be found in the book *De Bono's Course in Thinking*, London, BBC Publications; NY, Facts on File. A special CoRT CD can also be obtained via the web site.)

DATT

DATT stands for Direct Attention Thinking Tools. DATT is a special version of CoRT adapted to the world of work.

It was a handful of DATT tools that was taught to the illiterate miners in platinum mines in South Africa by Susan Mackie and Donalda Dawson. These were the tools that reduced disputes in the Karee mine from 210 a month to just four.

For training in the DATT method contact distributors listed on p. 287.

Parallel Thinking – the Six Thinking Hats

This framework is now very widely used around the world. It is used by top executives at some of the world's largest corporations (Siemens, British Telecom, Prudential, ABB, etc.) and by four-year-olds in school (Clayfield College, Brisbane, and the Low's School in Singapore). Simon Batchelor, on an aid mission to Cambodia, found himself teaching the framework to Khmer villagers to get them involved in water-drilling projects.

It is an alternative to traditional argument and is far more constructive. At any moment all thinkers involved are thinking in the same 'direction'. The direction is indicated by one or other of the six coloured hats. For example, the White Hat requires an attention to information: what do we have; what do we need; what is missing; how do we get what we need; what questions need to be asked? The Red Hat gives every thinker the opportunity to express feelings, emotions and intuition, without any need to explain or justify these. The Green Hat demands a focus on 'creative effort'. When the Green Hat is in use everyone makes a creative effort: new ideas, alternatives, modifications of an idea, possibilities, provocations, etc.

Experience has shown that Six Hat thinking is much more powerful and constructive than argument or discussion. It is also very much faster. Meeting times are reduced to one quarter or even one tenth.

The Six Hats method gets rid of egos, which are such a problem in traditional thinking. It is no longer a matter of defending an idea or attacking an idea. If you want to show off you do so by performing very well under each hat.

The Six Hat method is based on a consideration of how the brain chemicals differ when we are being cautious and when we are being positive. This chemical pre-sensitization is a key part of brain function. You cannot sensitize in all directions at once – so there is an absolute need to separate out the modes of thinking.

For formal training in the method, contact distributors listed on p. 287.

There is also the book *Six Thinking Hats*, London, Penguin Books; Boston, Mass., Little, Brown & Co.

Lateral Thinking

Creativity (in terms of new ideas and new perceptions) is not a mystical gift but a learnable skill. The formal and deliberate processes of lateral thinking are all based on a consideration of the behaviour of information in a self-organizing system, such as the nerve networks of the human brain. Such systems create routine patterns – for which we should be most grateful. They also form asymmetric patterns: the route from A to B is not the same as the route from B to A.

The formal techniques of lateral thinking include: provocation and movement; challenge; concept fans and concept triangles; random entry, etc. These processes are now widely used by designers, rock groups, strategists, etc. They are so powerful that in one afternoon one company (under the guidance of Carol Ferguson in South Africa) generated 21,000 ideas using just one technique. In Singapore, Peter and Linda Low ran a workshop from which came eight patents.

Formal training in these techniques is available; contact distributors listed on p. 287.

The book *Serious Creativity* (Harper Business and APTT) is the most up-to-date on the subject. Other books include *Lateral Thinking for Management*, London, Penguin Books.

Flowscapes

It is always very difficult to look at our own perceptions, because we cannot get outside ourselves.

Using the principles of 'water logic' we can, however, construct a map of our perceptions. We can then identify the central points into which other things feed. We can identify the repeating loops. We can see what points are peripheral – even if they had seemed central before.

We construct a 'flowscape' and then examine it.

The relevant book is *Water Logic*, London, Penguin Books; Des Moines, APTT.

Six Action Shoes

The starting-point for this framework was a lunch in London with some senior police officers. It was difficult to train people to deal with a variety of situations: paperwork; looking after a lost child; traffic duty; armed crime; domestic disputes; major disasters and crises, etc.

The Six Action Shoes separate action into six basic styles: such as 'routine action'; 'crisis action'; 'entrepreneurial action', etc. The action pattern for each style can be learned. It then becomes a matter, in training, of identifying the style – when you have to, you know what to do.

Unlike the Six Hats, the Action Shoes can be combined. There may be a crisis situation with high human values.

The relevant book is *Six Action Shoes* (originally published by Harper Business, NY). A formal training course is being prepared.

Other Books

Two other books which touch on these matters are:
Teach Your Child How to Think, London, Penguin Books; NY, Viking.
Teach Yourself to Think, London, Penguin Books.

Internet

The web site is www.edwdebono. com

There is a new message from me every week. The site sets projects and tasks from time to time. There are conference rooms for exchanging experiences. There are details of training courses. In all there are some seven hundred pages on the site.

Formal Training

Some years ago I set up a formal training programme because my work was being so messed around and distorted. For example, there were people teaching the Six Hats and insisting that at a meeting every person wore a different hat! This is almost exactly the opposite of the intended parallel thinking.

The formal training is organized by APTT. Trainers are certified either as independent trainers or as corporate trainers. In their training they use manuals which I have written. In this way I can be sure that the message is kept intact.

There are three formal programmes:

Six Hats

Lateral thinking

DATT

There are distributors in different countries. They should be contacted directly.

For training in DATT and the other programmes:

Europe: fax 44 (0)1494 868 787; e-mail holstgp@msn.com

Ireland: fax 353 1 8250

USA: fax 515 278 2245; www.innovatraining.com

Canada: fax 416 362 6422; www.micaworld.com

Other countries: fax (USA) 515 278 2245; www.aptt.com

Australia: contact de Bono Institute, Melbourne: Tel. 1 800 808 810; fax 03 9614 5344; e-mail max@debono org. Sydney: fax 02 9358 3475

Internet Courses

Quite separate from the formal training, it is envisaged that there will be individual courses run over the Internet. In due course these will be announced on the web site.

Software

Special software has been developed for lateral thinking. This is instructional, but also includes an 'Idea Processor' which can be used to generate ideas.

For sales and information contact **Australia**: 1 800 640 7330; fax 07 5491 9581

Video

2040
Lateral Thinking

Seminars

Information from The McQuaig Group
AIM in Australia
MCE in Brussels

Creative Retreats

Small groups of senior executives meet to think through strategies, concerns, opportunities and problems under the direct facilitation of Edward de Bono. Such meetings may be held on the island of Tessera in Venice, Little Green island in Queensland or elsewhere.

For further information on all the above contact:
Canada: The McQuaig Group, Toronto. Fax 416 488 4544. E-mail dmcquaig@debono.com
UK: Fax 44 171 602 1779
USA: APTT, Des Moines, Iowa. Fax: 1 515 278 2245

Ireland: Edward de Bono Foundation, Dublin. Fax 353 1 8250 467
Australia: The de Bono Institute, Melbourne. Tel. 1 800 808 810; fax 03 9614 5344; e-mail max@debono org
Sydney. Fax 02 9358 3475